THE
COLNE V_____
AND
HALSTEAD RAILWAY

by
R.A. Whitehead & F.D. Simpson

THE OAKWOOD PRESS

© The Oakwood Press 1988

First Edition 1951 (Francis Ridgway Ltd)
Second Edition 1987
Printed by Bocardo Press Ltd, Oxford
ISBN 0 85361 359 1

Acknowledgements

Elyot S. Hawkins, Esq., former General Manager of the Colne Valley
S.T. Scillitoe, Esq., the former Accountant
T.J. Rattee, Esq., recently Stationmaster, Halstead station
H.G. Hughes, Esq., Halstead
Editor of the *Halstead Gazette*
H.F. Hilton, Esq.,
K.A.C.R. Nunn, Esq.,
F.H. Smith, Esq.,
E.G. Axton, Esq.,
J.R. Hymas, Esq., Managing Director, Colne Valley Railway Coy, Ltd.

Published by
The OAKWOOD PRESS
P.O.Box 122, Headington, Oxford.

Contents

Bibliography

In the preparation of this history the following books and periodicals have been consulted:
The Railway Magazine
The Locomotive Magazine
The Halstead Gazette
The Halstead Times
Bradshaw's Guide
Old and New Halstead by William James Evans
The Stock Exchange Year Book
The Stock Exchange Official Intelligence
The Colne Valley & Halstead Railway (Arrangements) Act, 1885
The Great Eastern Railway Amalgamation Act, 1862
The Railway Year Book
Bradshaw's Shareholders' Guide, Railway Manual, and Directory
The Eastern Union Railway, by H.F. Hilton
History, Gazetteer and Directory of Essex by Wm. White
The Essex Almanac
The Colchester Gazette
The History of Public Transport in the Halstead Area: E.G. Axton. 1980
Great Eastern Railway Working and Public Time Tables, and Appendix thereto, *various.*

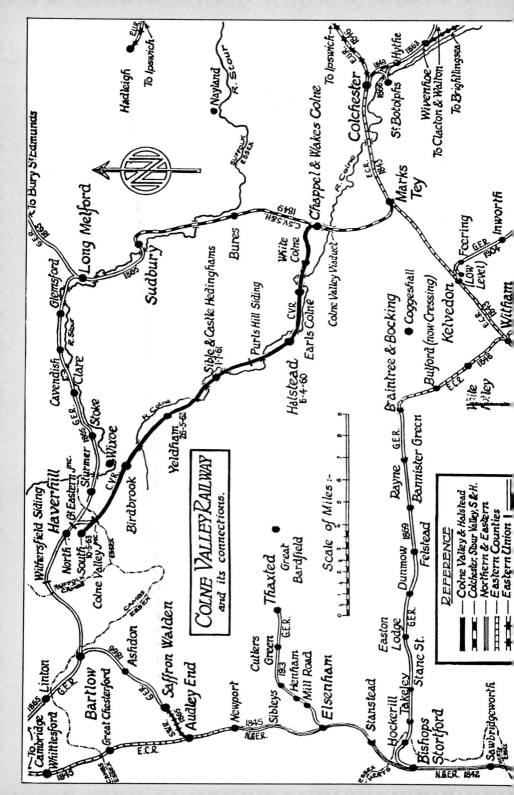

COLNE VALLEY RAILWAY and its connections.

Introduction

From very early days, railway companies tended to amalgamate. That this was only logical can be better appreciated if one considers the complications involved in making the journey from Felixstowe to Huntingdon, two stations no great distance apart on the old Great Eastern Railway, had the various portions of the route continued in the ownership of the seven or more undertakings by which they were constructed. Endless difficulties would have been encountered in attempting to arrange through train connections or fares between so many parties. Thus it was by amalgamation that the bigger railway systems as they existed in 1923 were built up, with the result that latterly, any small independent or separate railway line was generally of more than usual interest to railway enthusiasts, and of curiosity to others.

Relatively few of the smaller independent railways survived the 1923 grouping, so that only older generations can remember them from actual experience. Surely one of their most interesting features must have been the ever–present element of the unexpected. Trains would perhaps be composed of very curious rolling stock arrayed in diverse colours, headed by a locomotive of rather doubtful lineage, and sometimes of a distinctly unusual appearance.

It is for this reason that the authors feel that the life story of such undertakings should be recorded. Many have already had their histories written, and what an interesting story they have to tell! It is hoped therefore, that readers of this account of the birth, existence and final demise of a small East Anglian railway will not be disappointed. The authors hope too, that whilst younger readers may be able to recapture something of that spirit of individualism and independence that has characterized British industry in the past, older readers will have memories, both happy and otherwise, revived of their earlier travelling days.

The degree of interest the independent railway aroused varied enormously. Many achieved a certain fame, though not always of the kind the management would have preferred. Railways such as the Bishops Castle which never owned the land upon which its trains ran, and which broke all records by spending almost all of its long life in Chancery,—or the Hundred of Manhood and Selsey which ran two Model T Ford buses coupled back to back in an endeavour to compete with road competition. The 15″ gauge Eskdale could claim to be the world's smallest passenger railway until the advent of the Romney, Hythe and Dymchurch (almost the only line that has not been engulfed in the all–embracing British Railways). And what of the Easingwold? This little line of but 2¼ miles managed to enjoy a separate existence until 1948, and was unique in that it was still able to provide three classes of passenger accommodation, both smoking and otherwise, together with ample space for luggage, parcel traffic and the guard, within the compass of its two six–wheeled coaches. The Colne Valley cannot lay claim to fame on the score of the magnificence or otherwise of its passenger equipment—nor by reason of the peculiarity of the locomotives it employed (at any rate in its latter years) which probably accounts for the fact that it seems to have drawn little attention to itself in the shape of the written word or photographs taken during its lifetime. Nevertheless, the Colne Valley had a separate existence of 67 years which, though scarcely spectacular, was far from uneventful especially during its earlier years. If it had not been for the determined and public spirited manner in which some of the early Directors continued to find large sums of money, both for the completion and maintenance of the line, it must surely have passed out of existence long before. How the Colne Valley was able to reach the state of modest respectability it enjoyed in its latter years, after being in a state of utter financial chaos is truly amazing. Probably its only true claim to fame is that it survived at all, coupled with the facts that it never killed a single passenger in a train accident or paid a dividend!

Every endeavour has been made to ensure that all that is contained herein is accurate, but it is realized that in dealing with a subject in which human memory has to play quite a substantial part, some inaccuracies are bound to creep in. The authors therefore apologize for these in advance, and trust that any which may be discovered will be brought to their notice. They also hope that this short account will prove of interest not only to those whose living is in and about railways, and those many enthusiasts who make railways both full–scale and small–scale their hobby, but also to those who live or have lived in that very peaceful and charmingly rural valley in North Essex which gave its name to the subject of this book.

Readers will doubtless realize that it would not have been possible for a work of this nature to have reached completion without that very ready co–operation and assistance so gladly accorded the authors by the late London and North Eastern Railway, and in particular by the late Mr George Dow, the Company's Press Relations Officer at the time. There are many others to whom the authors are also indebted, and many sources have been consulted. As far as possible these are noticed in the Acknowledgements and Bibliography and to all who have assisted, whether mentioned or not, the writers offer their grateful thanks.

Introduction to the second enlarged edition

Some thirty–five years have passed since this little history was first written and went into print. There have since been many requests for copies of the book which has been out of print for some years. The Oakwood Press has now undertaken to re–issue the book under its imprint, and the opportunity has been embraced to take the story forward from 1923 when the Colne Valley and Halstead Railway passed into oblivion, at which point the original account closed. Details of the lines continuance under the London and North Eastern Railway through to its final demise at the hands of British Railways is now included.

Since publication of the first edition a considerable number of new photographs and other material have become available enabling a considerably enlarged illustrative content. This new edition now provides a complete account of this interesting railway which served north Essex for just over one hundred years before finally succumbing to the challenge of the automobile, whether it be car, lorry or motor–bus against which railway management seemed utterly unable to make the slightest positive move anywhere away from a prestige main-line.

R.A. Whitehead and
F.D. Simpson
1988

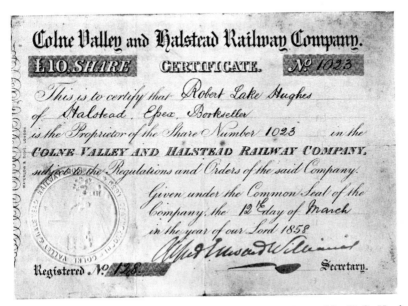

A reduced facsimile of an original £10 share certificate. *Loaned by H.G. Hughes*

7

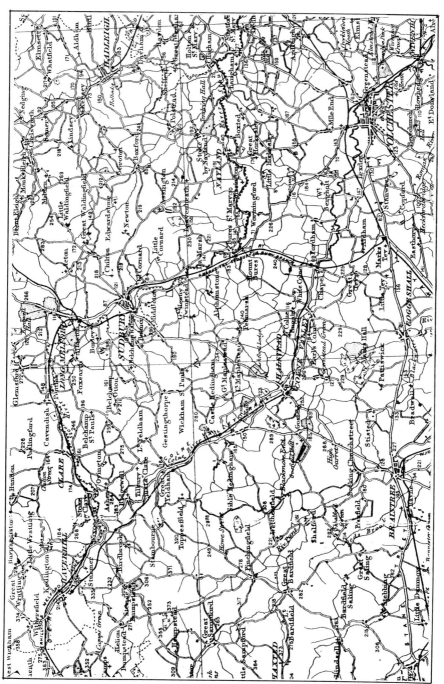

Reduced facsimile of Ordnance Survey map of the Colne Valley area: 1901
Outline edition.

Courtesy Ordnance Survey

Chapter One
1856—1864

The reputation enjoyed by the Eastern Counties Railway in the territory it served was not a thing that other companies might envy. The line was a butt for the humour of *Punch* and, what was worse, it had acquired a name for promising extensions and branches and subsequently forgetting its pledges. This was partly done with the idea of increasing the field from which capital might be gathered, but owing to the continued parlous state of its finances, largely the result of the "amicable" settlements arrived at with rapacious landowners and expensive and extravagant legal battles, scarely any of the subsidiary lines and branches in East Anglia were built by the Eastern Counties Railway. It seems to have been the definite policy of the Eastern Counties to adopt "obstructionism" towards any line outside its influence, to starve it into submission and then take it over on the harshest terms that the victim could be made to bear. The Eastern Counties gave notice in the Parliamentary session of 1846 of its intention to apply in the next session for powers to extend the Witham & Braintree branch to Halstead and apparently went as far as to submit plans and sections. Needless to say the line never materialized.

The first concrete project for providing railway facilities in the Colne Valley district came with the floating of the Colchester, Stour Valley, Sudbury and Halstead Railway in 1846, which was duly incorporated on 26th June of that year by Act 9 & 10 Vic., cap. 76. The original Act provided for a line from the Marks Tey station on the Eastern Counties Railway to Sudbury, with a branch to Halstead, 19 miles in all. In the following year powers were obtained to extend the line to Bury St. Edmunds, and to make a branch along the Stour Valley from Long Melford to Clare, bringing the total mileage up to 44 miles. The Company succeeded in constructing only the 12 miles of line between Marks Tey and Sudbury, which was not opened until 2nd July, 1849.

A short branch 1¼ miles long was constructed from the Eastern Union near Colchester to the Hythe, which line later became part of the Clacton branch. Hythe is the limit of navigation on the River Colne and forms the harbour for Colchester. Both this line and the Marks Tey – Sudbury branch were opened for passenger traffic on 2nd July, 1849, the latter including the Chappel viaduct, which is the largest in the county. It consists of 30 arches, each 35 feet span and 75 feet high. It cost £32,000 and over 7 million bricks were used in its construction.

The issued capital of the Colchester, Stour Valley, Sudbury and

Halstead – or Stour Valley for short – was £161,250, with loans of £32,360, in shares of £25, £15 paid.

It would seem that the Stour Valley, having no rolling stock of its own, approached the Ipswich and Bury Railway, and a lease for 999 years at £9,500 rent per annum was agreed. This was made legal by Act of June 7th, 1847, with the Eastern Union which had meanwhile absorbed the Ipswich and Bury. It seems that the terms were later revised upon the Stour Valley being fully incorporated into the Eastern Union which was to pay a rent equal to a guaranteed minimum of 5% on £83,000, together with a guaranteed minimum of 3% on the running cost of the line. It was further provided that whenever the Eastern Union paid its own "B" and "C" shareholders more than 5%, an equal sum should be paid on the £83,000, and whenever those shares received more than 3%, then an equal rate was to be paid on the remainder expended on the line, but in no case was more than 6% to be paid.

The Stour Valley obtained running powers over the Eastern Counties between Marks Tey and Colchester. From the commencement the line was worked by the Eastern Union which had built the line from Colchester to Ipswich following the failure of the Eastern Counties to carry its line on to Norwich.

The Halstead branch, and extensions to Bury St. Edmunds and Clare authorised by an Act in 1847 were never proceeded with, and the powers allowed to lapse until revived by the Great Eastern as will be seen later.

It is not surprising that the Eastern Union was never able to complete the Stour Valley for it was always hard pressed financially, on both capital and revenue accounts. After a great struggle it succeeded in completing its main line to Norwich, together with a few branches. On the revenue side, it never really had a fair chance, for the Eastern Counties Railway, on whom it was dependent for the handling of all its foreign traffic, made everything as difficult as possible. Finally, when the Norfolk Railway, with whom the Eastern Union had tried to form an alliance against the Eastern Counties, was safely enmeshed in the latter's ever expanding network, which touched all three terminal points[1] of the Eastern Union it was only a matter of time before it would find itself in the same position, having no other ally to turn to for assistance. So we find the Eastern Counties assuming the working of the Eastern Union system as from 1st January, 1854, though the company was not finally liquidated until the formation of the Great Eastern Railway in 1862.

Doubtless, the inhabitants and business folk of Halstead and the Colne Valley had high hopes that with the Sudbury line now forming part of the huge Eastern Counties system, something would soon be done to bring a railway into the Colne Valley, and Halstead in particular, its nearest station being 6 miles distant at Chappel. However, when 1856 came, there was still no sign of anything materializing, and bearing in mind the importance attached at that time to the possession of a railway service, it is not surprising to find the residents of the district taking matters into their own hands. It is perhaps, not unlikely, that the feeling prevalent towards the Eastern Counties Railway may have been an additional factor in the inception of the Colne Valley & Halstead Railway as an independent concern.

It was no small task for the inhabitants of such sparsely populated district, with very little industrial activity to take on, and even the Great Eastern Railway in its Guide of 1865, describing Halstead, condescended to pay the following compliment, namely: ". . . and had the spirit to carry out its own railway . . ." It has not been possible to trace the names of the persons who first mooted the subject, but the first Chairman was Mr Edward Hornor of The Howe, Halstead, so it may be assumed that some, at least, of the credit belongs to him. It would seem to be a fair assumption, also, that Mr James Brewster of Ashford Lodge, Halstead, played a fairly prominent part in the promotion of the line. Other members of the original Board of Directors were Mr Robert E. Greenwood, Mr John Hills and Mr Duncan Sinclair.

At first it was thought that Halstead might be best served by a line from Braintree, but this scheme was discarded – partly because of the difficulties of construction and partly because of the opposition of the Eastern Counties, Eastern Union and Colchester, Stour Valley, Sudbury & Halstead Railways – in favour of the scheme formally sanctioned by an Act of 30th June, 1856, which authorized the construction of a line from a junction with the Eastern Counties at Chappel to Halstead, to terminate at a point known as Parson's Bridge. A meeting was held in the Town Hall, Halstead on 25th July of the same year with the object of "promoting its immediate construction". The chair was taken by Mr Hornor. The capital of this original section of the line was £40,000, raised in £10 shares. The Engineer appointed was Mr Nathaniel Beardmore and the offices of Solicitor and Secretary were filled respectively by Mr Mayhew and Mr A.E. Williams. The first half-yearly meeting of the newly constituted company was held at the Town Hall on 29th September, 1856.

The necessary capital was raised with difficulty, and it was nearly 2 years before it was possible to make a start with the construction of the line. The first sod was cut by Mr Brewster in the presence of the principal officers of the Company and of the Contractor[2] Mr Munro at Elms Hall, the residence of Mr Mayhew, Solicitor to the Company, on

16th February, 1858. A local historian records that "the enthusiasm was not very great", only about fifty persons being present, including the interested parties already mentioned.

The work of construction proceeded steadily during the remainder of 1858 and throughout 1859. By the end of the latter year it was virtually complete with the exception of the junction with the Stour Valley (now owned by the Eastern Union but worked by the Eastern Counties) at Chappel, which had by that time proved to be a stumbling block. By a curious omission the Act incorporating the Colne Valley failed to make clear the manner in which this junction was to be constructed or the conditions to be imposed by the Stour Valley or its successors. The situation was obviously one in which the Eastern Counties held all the trump cards and they exploited the matter to the full. Numerous, protracted and, of course, quite fruitless meetings were held between their Engineer Mr Sinclair, and the Colne Valley's Engineer, Mr Beardmore. Eventually the difference was submitted to arbitration, involving the Colne Valley in considerable expense, the result of which, was an award requiring the Colne Valley to pay £1,500 for the right of entering the Chappel station and for the land they were to occupy. However, it was pointed out to the Colne Valley Board by their Solicitor, that the money should not be paid to the Eastern Counties who merely leased Chappel Station, but that the wisest course would be to pay the sum awarded into the Court of Chancery until such time as it could be decided who ought properly to receive it. The Board wisely followed this advice.

The Eastern Counties retaliated by a further period of inactivity until in desperation the Colne Valley applied to the Court of Common Pleas for a writ of mandamus requiring the Eastern Counties to state explicitly whether or not they intended to construct the junction. Meanwhile the Colne Valley Board appointed a sub-committee to negotiate with the Eastern Counties, and in the event of access to Chappel station being finally denied, it was empowered to construct a platform on Colne Valley property as near to the Eastern Counties station as possible. Under this pressure the Eastern Counties finally gave way to the extent of announcing that it would open the junction, and a series of meetings followed between the Colne Valley Chairman and Mr Love, Chairman of the Eastern Counties, as a result of which a basis of agreement was reached, one of the points the latter insisting upon being the annulment of the lease for working the line which had been granted to Mr Munro the contractor for construction. During one of the interviews Mr Love remarked that "Boards were not to be hurried . . . they were not very movable bodies . . . and that they required time for consideration"! At an earlier meeting of the Eastern Counties shareholders in connection with branch lines independently owned, Mr Love said "The duty of your Directors has been, when a line has been opened and is ready for working, to offer all reasonable facilities and on no account to interfere with the wishes of the public as regards the transit of goods. We hold this rule sacred". The hollowness of this high-flown nonsense was amply apparent to the Colne Valley.

It appears that the Eastern Counties did repent to the extent of loaning two of its largest locomotives for testing the Colne Valley track prior to opening. With minor exceptions Col. Yolland R.E., the Board of Trade Inspector, professed himself satisfied. The principal exception was the absence of a footbridge over the yard at Halstead which was rapidly remedied, a timber bridge being erected by Messrs Rayner and Runnacles in five weeks at a cost of £160; no mean feat for it will be seen from the station plan that it is a very long bridge. It has, however, long since been replaced by a steel bridge. However, while the work was in progress the Company decided to extend the line at the Halstead end to Trinity Street, a more central and accessible spot and the site of the present station, which was carried into effect by agreement with the Contractor. The work was completed in the spring of 1860, when the total length of line was 6 miles 2 chains, all of single track. The formal opening took place on Monday, 16th April, 1860, and the occasion was marked by the running of an excursion train to Colchester at a return fare of one shilling.

While this original portion of the line was yet under construction, schemes were discussed for an extension to Shelford, but after consideration, the decision was taken to extend the line to Haverhill, which town was still without a railway. The scheme for the additional line received Parliamentary sanction on 13th August, 1859. To cover the cost of these further works, the ordinary share capital was increased by £43,000, again in £10 shares.

The first sod of the extension was turned on June 19th, 1860 by Miss Gurteen of Haverhill, a member of the family long established in that town as cotton goods manufacturers and whose mills today form the principal source of employment in the town. The scene of the ceremony was a field some two miles from Haverhill, owned, the report tells us, by a Mrs Walton. The railway had by this time drawn more attention upon itself than it had when Mr Brewster carried out his spade work at Elms Hall two years before and the account remarks that "there were about 2,000 people present and great enthusiasm prevailed". Apparently the enthusiasm was not confined to the local populace for the ninth half yearly report, issued in September 1860, blithely informed the shareholders that it was hoped that the line would be open as far as Hedingham by Christmas. The

Directors were careful to avoid stating to which Christmas they referred!

At the tenth half yearly meeting of the Company, early in 1861, the directors had to report that through no fault of the Contractor the section to Hedingham had not been completed as expected. The Chairman allocated part of the blame to the weather which, he said, had been particulary inclement about Christmas time but expressed the hope that Mr Munro would make up for lost time and have the section open in two months. Part of the blame, however, he reserved for landowners, some of whom apparently had not given possession of the necessary land as readily as they might have done and he appealed to them so to do in order that construction might not be delayed.

During 1860 a number of changes had taken place among the functionaries of the line. Mr Brewster succeeded Mr Hornor as Chairman and on 22nd August, Mr Joseph Cubitt became Engineer for the Haverhill extension. Another change in the latter part of the year was the resignation of Mr Williams, the Secretary, he being succeeded by Mr Edmund Harvey. The tenth half-yearly meeting, to which reference has already been made, revealed that he received the sum of £100 per annum for his exertions. It was proposed by the Directors that they be granted power to increase this salary at their discretion to a limit of £500 per annum. The meeting, however, refused to sanction such an "excessively" high limit and after some oratorical thrusts the Directors lowered the limit to £300 per annum, to which more moderate demand the assembly gave its consent. Mr Brewster, who was in the chair at the meeting, was a somewhat "piquant" personality and it is probable, therefore, that the situation was at times a little stormy.

On Monday, 24th June, 1861, the line as far as Hedingham was ready for inspection by the Board of Trade Inspector. The inspector who officiated on this occasion was again Col. Yolland, R.E.; he was favoured by the attendance of Mr R.E. Greenwood, a Director, Mr Munro, the Contractor, Mr R.J. Watt, the Manager and Mr C.B. Sperling, the sub-Engineer. The only point to which the Colonel took exception was the absence of a siding at Hedingham, the provision of which he considered to be a necessity and the following Thursday the *Halstead Gazette* was happy to report that "the Colonel has expressed himself satisfied and that the necessary certificate will forthcoming as soon as Mr Cubitt has furnished one testifying to the completion of the above-mentioned siding".

In the next issue it was able to carry the glad news of the opening to the populace in the following words:

Monday, the 1st of July, was another eventful day in the history of Halstead – our Colne Valley Railway was opened to the public as far as

Castle Hedingham. The iron road has not only reached but shot beyond the town and as it carries in its wake the elements of opening out, beautifying and enriching a country, so it leaves in its train (sic!) those advantages extended and consolidated and more – in proportion to the extent of feeder lines that run right and left of the special locality . . . The shareholders have cause to congratulate themselves on the accomplishment of an effort their children's children will boast of, and on the possession of a property that we doubt not will very shortly be remunerative.

From the remainder of the greater part of two columns devoted to the event we learn that the inhabitants of Halstead "were roused from the even tenor of their ways by a merry peal from the church tower, a fluttering of flags and the inspiring strains of the brass band of the 12th Essex Rifles" but that the Hedinghams remained aloof, with the exception of a Mr C. Hilton, who went to the trouble of decorating the railway bridge there, and at whose expense the band of the 12th Essex Rifles was engaged.

Cheap fares were provided for the benefit of the celebrants, the return fare from Hedingham to Halstead being 4d. and to Chapel 6d. No extra trains were run for the day and the booked trains were, as a result, packed to overflowing, and cattle trucks had to be pressed into service to accommodate the remaining passengers. In all some 1,700 people travelled, 700 from Halstead itself. The return journey from Chappel was made an hour late owing to the difficulty of "reassembling and reseating those who thought to avail themselves of a longer stay there than had been prescribed". Surprisingly enough no mishaps were reported. The prevailing feeling of goodwill toward the line is, perhaps, best summed up by the slogan "Progress and Prosperity" which the town of Halstead displayed on an arch of evergreens spanning the level crossing at Trinity Street.

The construction of the section from Castle Hedingham to Yeldham was carried on through the remainder of the summer and autumn of 1861 without incident but the winter again hindered the execution of the works, mainly through heavy rains, as a result of which an accident occurred in a cutting near Yeldham on the 10th January, 1862. A fall of about 5 tons of earth took place, burying two labourers, Henry Bunton and John Watkinson, and injuring a third, Thomas Ruggles. The two men were extricated in about half an hour, but Bunton was dead when found, Watkinson dying soon afterwards. Ruggles escaped with an injury to his leg.

It would seem that from the date of opening, traffic at the Halstead terminal was handled without any station buildings[3] whatever and it has not been possible to find any mention of even a temporary structure. In the issue of the *Halstead Gazette* for 6th February, 1862, however, the Company invited tenders for the construction of a station at Halstead to the design and specification of Mr Cubitt, which were published a fortnight later. The building described is the present station and the specification required it to be "built of white stock bricks, facings to be of blue, red and terra cotta patent bricks". The platform was to be "covered in with a handsome awning of corrugated zinc and plate glass, supported by six handsome iron columns". The description would almost exactly fit the building today, except for the awning, although opinions have changed on the question of architectural design. A building regarded as admirable eighty years ago would not necessarily pass as such today. The successful contractors were Messrs Rayner and Runnacles, the amount of whose tender was £2,730 and it must be conceded that, whatever the aesthetic merit of the building, it was a very sound piece of construction.

The extension to Yeldham was opened on 26th May, 1862, ten months after the opening to Hedingham. There was a good deal of celebration but not that exhuberance which characterised the opening of the previous section. Possibly it was felt that after the efforts of that occasion any similar attempt would seem paltry by comparison or, possibly, other excitements may have diverted attention from it.

The completion of the remaining portion of line to Haverhill occupied the best part of another year, despite the Contractors' employing some 300–400 men on the task. The first train entered Haverhill on the 10th May, 1863, using a temporary station pending the completion of the buildings there. These included a repair shop and running shed for locomotives. The repair facilities were not of a very elaborate nature, however, as will be noticed later.

At the opening of the line, the motive power comprised the two small tank engines used by Mr Munro, the Contractor, but these were shortly superseded by a second-hand tank engine from the London, Brighton & South Coast Railway, and an 0–6–0 tender goods engine from the Eastern Counties Railway, which were used until the arrival early in 1861 of the first of three new Manning, Wardle tank engines. A separate chapter gives full details of these and other locomotives owned by the Company.

The completion of the line between Chappel and Haverhill was overshadowed as far as the company was concerned by a dispute which had arisen with the Eastern Counties Railway and which eventually made the Colne Valley the scene of a struggle between two major companies, the Eastern Counties and the London & North Western. We have already noticed that the Eastern Counties bestowed little favour upon any schemes for branches promoted within its sphere of influence and its attitude towards the Colne Valley was

Mr Elyot S. Hawkins, last General Manager of the CV&H Railway photographed in 1917 whilst serving with King's Shropshire Light Infantry.
Authors' Collection

Wooden panel with Armorial device of the CV&H Railway. *Authors' Collection*

Portraits of five of the early Directors of the line.
J. Brewster 1807–1890
E. Hornor 1811–1868
J.R. Vaizey 1840–1900
George de Horne Vaizey 1800–1873
R.E. Greenwood   *Authors' Collection*

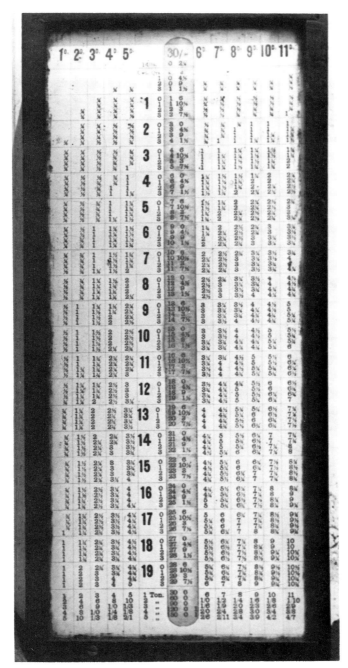

An interesting Passenger, Parcels and Goods Rates Calculator used at CV&H Railway stations, this one photographed at Yeldham. *Authors' Collection*

The three bogie carriages acquired from the Metropolitan District Railway used for the electric traction experiments seen here as delivered and looking extremely smart, at Halstead Station.

Authors' Collection

Above
Up home and down starter signal on the same mast at Birdbrook, notice spectacle glass separated from its arm. The train for Haverhill has just departed.   *P.J. Kelley*

Above right
Ex-GER down starter at Earls Colne: note the acute angle of the signal arm, a common feature of GE signals.   *P.J. Kelley*

Right
Up distant signal at Birdbrook with lower spectacle.   *P.J. Kelley*

Haverhill North showing the exterior frontage. This was a standard GER design in the 1860s to be found all over the system, with station master's house placed end on to platform, centre section with entrance awning and booking office and waiting rooms, and porters, lamp and store rooms, parcel office etc., on the right. The pleasing use of contrasting bricks for the door and window openings, with stringing courses makes a very worthy structure.   *Authors' Collection*

Ex-GER Junction signals at Haverhill. The centre arm for Sudbury line, the right one is for the CV line: calling on arm for refuge siding on left: the siding on right was used by CV trains waiting for departure time.   *P.J. Kelley*

Haverhill North station viewed towards Sudbury in 1947 showing the station house and garden, and the goods shed in the distance. Combine harvesters on trucks are to be seen in the loading dock. *Authors' Collection*

A further view of Haverhill North station looking towards Cambridge . The footbridge is of standard GER pattern but has lost its roof. *Authors' Collection*

Haverhill. Hamlet Road viaduct carrying link line from GE station to Colne Valley Junc. (CV). This is now the subject of a preservation Order.

Authors' Collection

Haverhill Station looking to the end of the line (seen here on an old postcard) showing the platform and modest station building. Considerable changes have been effected later, as the carriage shed and cattle pens have been moved, and there is a siding curving away to the right along the platform. The goods shed still has its doors, and there is an ancient brake van body on the left.

Lens of Sutton

Haverhill Stⁿ, Goods Shed, and Carriage Shed

no exception to this policy. When early in the history of the line the Directors approached the Eastern Counties with a view to securing its consent to the construction of the Colne Valley their efforts met with a very lukewarm reception and it soon became apparent that little co-operation would be forthcoming.

In an atmosphere of this kind it is not surprising that the Colne Valley company sought to make itself independent of its unaccommodating neighbour. There were other powerful railway interests at Cambridge and it was in this direction that the Colne Valley Board looked for another outlet. So it came about, that a Bill was presented to Parliament in 1860, in which the proposals broadly consisted of extending the line at one end to Cambridge and at the other to Colchester, thus providing a very useful cross-country line.

From the first the Bill encountered the vehement opposition of the Eastern Counties who had in the same session lodged Bills for the construction of lines from Sudbury to Bury St Edmunds with a branch from Long Melford to Clare, thus reviving the powers obtained by the Colchester, Stour Valley, Sudbury & Halstead in 1847 which had long since lapsed; and for a new line from Clare to Shelford station on the Eastern Counties main line from London to Cambridge. The Colne Valley Bill at one juncture appeared likely to fail under Standing Orders and petitions from the Mayors, Aldermen and Burgesses of Colchester and Cambridge were presented praying that it should not be set aside until next session. The petitions were evidently not without effect for the Bill was declared to comply with Standing Orders and the company were given leave to proceed with it. On 7th March, 1861 the *Halstead Gazette* reported that the Bill had passed its second reading in the Commons and had passed the Standing Orders of the Lords. It should be noted in passing that the Eastern Counties proposals meant the construction of a line practically parallel to the Colne Valley, effectively preventing it from participating in any through traffic from points west of Haverhill to points east of Chappel.

The objectors to the Eastern Counties Bill were given by the *Railway Times* as the Stour Valley, the Norfolk, the Eastern Union and the Colne Valley Railways. It is a little difficult to see why the first three lines should be entered as objectors since they were already within the Eastern Counties fold. The same source give the objectors to the Colne Valley Bill as Stour Valley (which had already been taken over by the Eastern Union Railway twelve years previously!) the Bedford and Cambridge (an abortive offshoot of the Eastern Counties Railway), and the Norfolk and Eastern Union Railways – both of which had already been absorbed by the Eastern Counties Railway, which

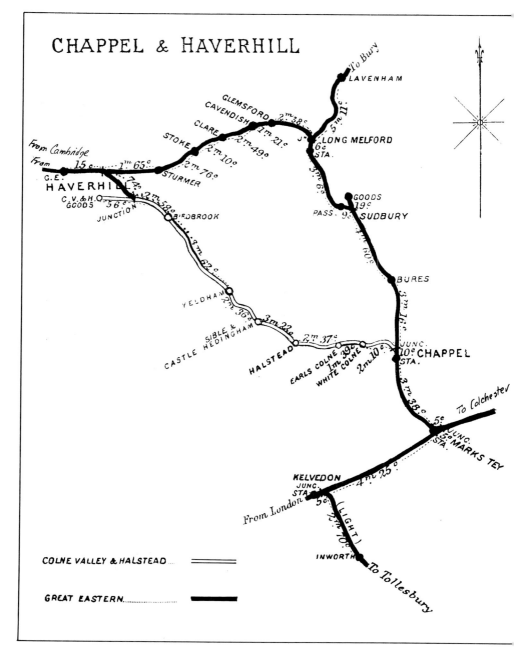

A map of the CV&H Railway as it appeared in the Railway Clearing House book of Official Railway Junction Diagrams (1915 edition) showing the intermediate distances in miles and chains.

latter was also entered as an objector. The opposition was thus really one and the same.

The Bills came up for consideration in Committee on 13th May, 1861, the Parliamentary Committee being under the Chairmanship of Mr Mowbray. The counsel were Mr Sargeant Wrangham, Mr Denison and Mr J. Clark for the Colne Valley, Mr Hope Scott, Mr O. Merewether and Mr Burke for the Eastern Counties and Sir F. Slade, Mr Wilkinson and Mr Hayley for the Eastern Union and Norfolk Railways, which were opposing both Bills. The title of the Colne Valley Bill disclosed that its purpose was to enable the Colne Valley and Halstead Railway to extend their line to Cambridge, Clare and Colchester and for other purposes. From the opening speech of Mr Sargeant Wrangham it became clear that one of the "other purposes" was to enable the completed undertaking to be leased to the London & North Western Railway and that the London & North Western were prepared to contribute toward the capital cost. It is thus easy to understand the Eastern Counties' desire to stop the Bill at almost any cost.

The schemes of the Colne Valley which the learned counsel set forth comprised a line from Haverhill to Cambridge 16 miles 6 furlongs in length; a line from Chappel to Colchester 7 miles 3 furlongs in length and a branch from Birdbrook, between Yeldham and Haverhill, to Wixoe and Clare, 4 miles 2 furlongs in length. He further referred to the unconciliatory attitude of the Eastern Counties towards the Colne Valley in its early days; to its opposition to the Bill for the Colne Valley extension of 1859 and to the delicate mixture of detestation and derision with which the former was regarded by the local inhabitants. His arguments failed to convince the Committee, however, and to the chagrin of the Colne Valley its Bill was rejected while that of the Eastern Counties duly became law, being passed by the House of Lords on 22nd July, 1861.

This setback did not deter the Colne Valley & Halstead Railway from promoting a further Bill in the session of 1863 with similar but more limited objects. It proposed to construct a line from a junction at Haverhill with the Eastern Counties line already under construction to link up with the Clare and Shelford line (mentioned in the last paragraph) in the adjoining parish of Withersfield, and a branch from Birdbrook to a junction with the Clare and Shelford line in the parish of Wixoe. It further proposed to compel the abandonment of the Eastern Counties line between the points mentioned and also to abandon their Haverhill branch. This time the Company were more successful and were granted the statutory authority to build the new lines. The proposals, however, had several obvious drawbacks, which left the Colne Valley dependent on the Great Eastern Railway (as the Eastern Counties had then become) and gave it no independent access to either Colchester or Cambridge. The latter omision was of particular importance as it meant that the London & North Western Railway was no longer interested and that its financial support was, therefore, withdrawn. With this powerful aid lost the Colne Valley found it impossible to finance their new venture and from lack of funds it was allowed to lapse.

Although not able to have their own line to Cambridge, it would seem that the Colne Valley was anxious to get the anticipated Cambridge traffic developing as soon as possible, for the following advertisement appeared in the *Colchester Gazette* dated 6th May, 1864:

COLNE VALLEY RAILWAY

This Company invites TENDERS from Post Masters, Coach Proprietors and others to provide and work an OMNIBUS daily (Sundays excepted) to and from HAVERHILL & CAMBRIDGE.

Parties tendering are requested to state terms, per month, they will undertake the service until August next, or to such time as the Great Railway Company's Extension is opened to Cambridge.

The Company are willing to give a subsidy for the proper performance of the service.

Tenders to be forwarded to the undersigned on or before the 16th. inst.

Halstead, Essex. May 2nd, 1864.

JN. B. COOPER,
Manager.

The Authors have not discovered whether such Omnibus service was in fact provided.

When the Great Eastern opened their line from Shelford to Haverhill on 1st June, 1865, the Colne Valley made an attempt to secure running powers to Cambridge one way and Colchester and Harwich the other, but again the proposals came to nothing. The disputes with the Great Eastern dragged on sporadically and as late as 1869 we find that the Colne Valley still had sufficient differences with that company to warrant their submission to the Arbitration of a Mr Tyler. Gradually, however, the troubles diminished with a more enlightened management on the Great Eastern Railway and co-operation took their place.

The only link in the Colne Valley undertaking of which the construction remains to be recorded is a connecting line between it and the Great Eastern station at Haverhill, built to enable traffic to be interchanged. This line commences with a junction nearly three-quarters of a mile short of the Colne Valley station, and joins the

Great Eastern about a quarter of a mile east of its Haverhill station. Work on this link was commenced by the Great Eastern Railway in 1864, under the supervision of Mr C.B. Sperling, the Colne Valley & Halstead Engineer, on behalf of his Company, and it was completed and opened at the same time as the Great Eastern line from Haverhill to Sudbury on 9th August, 1865. Upon the completion of this line the Colne Valley trains used the Great Eastern station except where there was no connecting train, in which case, usually the last train of the day, the Colne Valley station was used.

[1] Colchester, Bury St. Edmunds and Norwich.

[2] The Eastern Counties had offered to construct the line at prime cost, an offer the Board wisely declined.

[3] Nathaniel Beardmore's report of 24th February, 1860 says *inter alia*, . . . the Halstead station is nearly ready for the purpose of any present opening of your line; the corrugated iron engine and goods sheds have been some time in hand, and will be completed within a month.

Extract from *The Essex Almanac* of 1905 detailing the principal functionaries of the line.

Chapter Two
1865—1922

The cessation of hostilities with the Great Eastern did not mark the end of strife so far as the Colne Valley & Halstead was concerned. No sooner had external troubles lessened than certain internal differences manifested themselves, which are dealt with more fully later.

The working of the line was carried out by the Company from the opening date until the end of 1864 under the supervision of Mr Robert Johnston Watt as Traffic Manager (except from a short time in 1863–64 when a Mr Cooper was Manager) and Mr C.B. Sperling as Engineer. Financially this method of working was not altogether successful, and from 1st January, 1865 the working was leased to Sir Daniel Gooch. Mr Munro, the contractor for the construction, had twice offered to lease the line, once in 1859 and again in 1863 while in 1862 we find recorded in the Minutes of the Board Meeting a draft agreement for a lease to a Mr Birkbeck, which also came to nothing. Gooch placed a Mr Rogers in the post of Manager, and Mr Watt, of whom we shall hear more later, departed for fresh fields. Gooch continued to work the line until 31st December, 1866. From the 1st January to 15th June, 1867 the lease was taken over by Mr Sperling, the Company's former Engineer, and after that for a short time by Mr Watt, who had reappeared on the scene. Finally, in the latter half of the year it reverted to the Colne Valley and Messrs Watt and Sperling resumed their respective posts as General Manager and Engineer.

Local opinion and the local Press was divided at that time into two camps, pro-railway and anti-railway, or more accurately, pro-Watt and anti-Watt. There were two competitive newspapers published in Halstead – the *Halstead Gazette* and the *Halstead Times* which supported the two respective factions. It is not possible after the lapse of years to form any fair judgment on the continuous blast and counter-blast of correspondence, charges and counter-charges which appeared in these newspapers for some years, and which are almost the only surviving signs of the controversy. The *Halstead Times* was particularly conspicuous in its disparagement of the Colne Valley, and more especially with the execration of Mr Watt and all his works. The authors have been privileged to read through some notes left by the late Mr Hughes, Editor of the *Halstead Times*, from which it can be inferred that he was endowed with an impish sense of humour – lacking in the opposition – and that much was written with his tongue in his cheek.

It would seem that things got so bad that the *Colchester Gazette* of 16th September, 1864, said the local Bench had decided to publish certain portions of the Libel Law, hoping the warning would cause those responsible for the spate of defamatory proceedings to stop. Mr

86.—COLNE VALLEY AND HALSTEAD.

Incorporated by 19 and 20 Vic., cap. 61 (30th June, 1856), to make a railway from the Chappel station of the Colchester and Stour Valley to the town of Halstead, in the county of Essex. Capital, 40,000*l.*, in 10*l.* shares; loans, 13,333*l.*

Agreement may be made with the Colchester and Stour Valley and Great Eastern. Length, 6¼ miles, forming a junction with Colchester and Stour Valley. Opened 16th, April, 1860.

By 22 and 23 Vic., cap. 122 (13th August, 1859), the company was authorised to extend the line from Halstead to Haverhill. New capital, 80,000*l.* in shares, and 26,000*l.* on loan. Open to Castle Hedingham, 3¼ miles, 1st July, 1861; to Yeldham, 2½ miles, on 26th May, 1862; to Haverhill, 10th May, 1863. In operation, 20 miles.

By 24 and 25 Vic., cap. 237 (6th August, 1861), the company was authorised to raise additional capital to the extent of 30,000*l.* in shares, and 10,000*l.* on loan.

By the Amalgamation Act of 1862 the Great Eastern is bound to take and work the Colne Valley, if the company call upon them to do so, on the terms of paying over 50 per cent. of the earnings. Facilities are also given for transmission and receipt of traffic between the Colne Valley and the Great Eastern, by through booking and through rates, in case the former company should prefer to work its own line.

By 26 and 27 Vic., cap. 186 (21st July, 1863), the company was authorised to increase its capital by 28,000*l.* in shares at 5 per cent., and 9,000*l.* on loan. An agreement for joint use of the Great Eastern station at Haverhill, with running powers thereto, was also sanctioned.

By 28 Vic., cap 1 (7th April, 1865), the company was authorised to raise new capital to the extent of 40,000*l.* in shares and 13,300*l.* on loan.

The Colne Valley and Halstead was handed over on the 1st January, 1865, to Daniel Gooch, Esq., M.P., on a working contract, terminable upon giving him six month's notice, upon terms of paying over to the company 35 per cent. of the gross receipts. In May, 1865, at a meeting of bondholders the following gentlemen were chosen to represent debenture holders, Mr. Upton, Mr. Pigeon; construction bondholders and judgment creditors, Mr. Green, Mr. Childs; shareholders, Mr. Mayhew, to co-operate with and assist the directors in developing the resources of the company.

The traffic account furnished by Mr. Gooch for the half-year ending 30th June gave a total receipt of 4,438*l.* Under the terms of the contract, 35*l.* per cent. is payable to the company, and gives a sum of 1,553*l.*, available towards interest for the current half-year, but this sum appeared to the directors to be too small to propose a division.

This gross receipt of 4,438*l.* is an increase as compared with the corresponding half-year of 1864, which amounted to 3,890*l.*

CAPITAL.—This account to 30th June furnishes the subjoined detail of income and expenditure :—

Received.		*Expended.*	
Ordinary shares	£62,618	Preliminary	£6,605
Preference shares—Less rebate of		Extension act, 1859	3,669
23,680*l.*	65,580	Preliminary, 1861	6,393
Debentures	56,714	Preliminary, 1863	1,802
Construction Bonds	76,200	Land and compensation	37,677
Balance	1,523	Works—construction	149,567
		Engineer	10,260
		Electric telegraph works	837
		Secretary	250
		Permanent way and works	1,958
		Plant and rolling stock	9,695
		Chappel Junction award	1,500
		Interest on loans	21,623
		Stations	4,711
		Direction and audit	2,809
		General charges	3,373
	£262,636		£262,636

Meetings in February and August.

No. of Directors—6; minimum, 3; quorum, 3. *Qualification*, 250*l.*

DIRECTORS:

Chairman—JAMES BREWSTER, Esq., Ashford Lodge, Halstead, Essex.

R. E. Greenwood, Esq., Sloe House, Halstead, Essex.

Robt. Chas. Hanam, Esq., 1, Alderman's Walk, Bishopsgate Street, London, E.C.

Edgar Corrie, Esq., 26, Lombard Street, London, E.C.

Fred. Payne, Esq., Wixoe, Haverhill.

George Gamble, Esq., Bedford Place, Russell Square, Bloomsbury, London, W.C.

OFFICERS.—Man., R. Rogers, Halstead; Sec., Edmund Harvey, 6, Victoria Street, Westminster. S.W.; Eng., Joseph Cubitt, C.E., 6, Great George Street, Westminster, S.W.; Auditors, W. H. Wilson, 6, Victoria Street, Westminster, S.W., and A. J. Browne, Halstead; Solicitors, Baxter, Rose, Norton, and Co., 6, Victoria Street, Westminster, S.W.

Secretary's Office—6, Victoria Street, Westminster Abbey, London, S.W.

Particulars of the Company as detailed in Bradshaw's *Railway Shareholders Manual* of 1866.

Brewster, the Colne Valley Chairman, was also a local Justice of the Peace!

In 1862, the Company was successful in obtaining the insertion of a clause in the Great Eastern Amalgamation Act, making it incumbent upon the latter to take over the working of the railway for 50% of the receipts, should the Colne Valley so decide at any time. This right was never exercised, but it had a certain value as a lever against any hostile intentions on the part of the Great Eastern, since it would obviously have been against the latter's interest to injure the Colne Valley who could at any time invoke this clause.

We must here digress for a moment to consider the parlous state into which the Company's finances had drifted. Briefly the capital account may be summarized as follows:

Shares

Date	Description	Amount Authorised	Amount Issued
1856	Ord.	£40,000	
1859	Ord.	£80,000	£61,200 Ord.
†1861	Ord.	£30,000	£72,380 Pref.
1863	Pref.	£28,000	£11,870
1865	Ord. or Pref.	£40,000	
Position in 1865		£218,000	£145,450*

Loans

Date	Amount Authorised	Amount Issued
1856	£13,333	–
1859	£26,000	–
1861	£10,000	–
1863	£9,000	£57,745 3 8
1865	£13,300	–
	£71,633	£57,745 3 8

* As to £61,200 Ordinary £84,250 Preference.
† The Act of 1861 authorised a preferential dividend on the balance of £88,800 shares previously authorised but not issued.

No dividend was ever paid on the Ordinary Shares and nothing was paid on the Preference Stock after 1864. The foregoing table does not represent the sum total of the Company's commitments; Mr Munro, the Contractor, having agreed to accept 5% Construction Bonds to the nominal value of £76,200 in lieu of cash, a highly

irregular though far from uncommon practice subsequently pro-
hibited by Act of Parliament. No interest was paid on these bonds
after 1864. Even this vast amount of capital was insufficient to meet
the Company's most pressing engagements so a further sum of
£50,000 was borrowed from Mr Robert Tweedy and Mr James
Brewster, as security for which they received 6,000 of the unissued
£10 Preference shares. Later the holders of these shares obtained a
judgment against the railway for £40,612 5s. 6d. while the holders of
certain of the Statutory Bonds and Construction Bonds also secured
judgments for the amounts due to them.

The final blow came on the 19th November, 1874, when Mr James
Brewster, acting for himself and other bond-holders, made a successful application to the Court of Chancery for the appointment of a
receiver, the Secretary, Mr W.G. Bailey, being appointed to that
position.

The Receivership lasted eleven years and during that time a slow
but steady improvement took place. The year 1876 saw the purchase
of a new 0–4–2 tank locomotive from Messrs Neilson, while the next
year marked the final departure of Mr Watt, the General Manager, Mr
John Crabtree taking his place. The first of a series of improvements
following his appointment was the purchase of a second-hand 0–6–0
tank locomotive (*Haverhill*).

It would appear that from 1864 up to this time the Company never
owned the rolling stock used on the line, for in 1864 the whole of it
was sold to Robert Tweedy of Truro for £9,010. The later locomotives
and rolling stock were hired from Mr C.E. Brewster, but on 9th April,
1877, they were valued at £6,547 and a Court Order decreed that from
the 4th May, 1878, that sum was to be paid to Mr Brewster at the rate
of £1,200 per annum, plus 5% interest on the balance, the vehicles to
remain his property until all was paid.

After nearly six years service with the Colne Valley Mr Crabtree
departed in 1882 to take up his appointment as General Manager of
the new Great Northern & Great Eastern Joint Railway. Mr George
Copus became the new General Manager and he found the motive
power department still sadly wanting. An ex-North London Railway
0–4–2 saddle tank engine was purchased to help meet the shortage
and in 1887 a steam travelling crane was added.

It was obvious that a straightening-out of the finances was long
overdue and in July 1883 a Committee of Bondholders was set up
with this object. Unfortunately the Committee could not agree with
the Directors as to the best method of accomplishing the task so that
in 1884 the Colne Valley and Halstead Railway (Arrangements) Bill
was referred to a Committee of the House of Lords who found it
inexpedient to proceed with it.

50.—COLNE VALLEY AND HALSTEAD.

Incorporated by act of 30th June, 1856, to make a railway from the Chappel Station of the Colchester and Stour Valley to the town of Halstead, in the county of Essex.

Agreement with Colchester and Stour Valley and Great Eastern.

By the Amalgamation Act of 1862, the Great Eastern is bound to take and work the Colne Valley, if the company call upon them to do so, on the terms of paying over 50 per cent. of the earnings. Facilities are also given for transmission and receipt of traffic between the Colne Valley and the Great Eastern, by through booking and through rates, in case the former company should prefer to work its own line.

Powers for extension, &c., were obtained under acts 1859, 1861, 1863, 1865, and 1885.

By act of 14th August, 1885, powers were obtained to re-constitute the board of directors, refer the affairs of the company to arbitration, and to borrow a sum not exceeding 50,000l. as a first mortgage in priority to any of the company's borrowed or other capital, being a first charge upon the undertaking and its gross receipts, after payment of working and maintenance, annual rent-charges, and all rates, taxes, or other burdens affecting the same.

With reference to the arbitrations referred to above, the company's report issued in March, 1886, stated as follows:—

Under the act." the Right Hon. Lord Bramwell was appointed arbitrator, who has by virtue of it made two awards—one a preliminary award dated 21st November, 1885, with reference to the future government of the company; the other and final award, dated 11th February, 1886.

"By these awards his lordship has authorised the company to raise by pre-preference debenture stock (subject only to the rent-charges, amounting to 96l. per annum) the sum of 50,000l., to be called 'A' debenture stock, and has further converted the existing statutory bonds, construction bonds, and judgment debts, together with existing arrears thereon, amounting altogether to 367,365l., into 'B' debenture stock. The 'B' debenture stockholders are not to be entitled to any dividend except out of the net earnings of each year, thereby rendering any future arrears on that stock impossible. The arbitrator has then awarded that the net income of the company, after payment of the rent-charges and interest on the 'A' debenture stock, shall be applied first in paying interest on the 'B' debenture stock until 1 per cent. has been paid. If there be any further moneys applicable to dividend, it shall be divided between the 'B' debenture stock and the preference and ordinary shares in such manner as that the 'B' debenture stock shall receive thereout twice as much per cent. as the preference shares, and the preference shares twice as much as the ordinary shares.

"The arbitrator has further consolidated the two classes of preference stocks (the second of which was only 1,750l. in amount), and limited the maximum dividends receivable by the 'B' debenture stockholders to 4 per cent., and those receivable by the preference shareholders to 5 per cent."

Under the Regulation of Railways Act, 1889, the sum of 12,150l. was authorised to be raised.

In operation, 19 miles.

CAPITAL.—The receipts and expenditure on this account to 30th June, 1895, were detailed as follow:—

Received.		Expended.	
Ordinary shares	£61,200	Parliamentary and preliminary expenses	£19,163
Preference shares	25,590	Land and compensation, works, engineering, permanent way, interest, stations, and plant	269,293
"A" debenture stock	58,806		
"B" debenture stock	367,365		
Balance	3,251	Direction, audit, and office expenses	6,240
		Additional capital created in payment of interest on statutory and construction bonds and judgment debts	159,458
		Reconstruction account	50,238
		Regulation of Railways Act, 1889	11,820
	£516,212		£516,212

REVENUE.—No dividend is being paid at present on the preference and ordinary shares, but the dividend on the 5 per cent. "A" debentures is regularly paid. A dividend of 2s. 6d. per cent. on the "B" debenture stock was paid for the year ended 31st December, 1892. The balance in favour of revenue account carried to general balance sheet for the half-year ended 30th June, 1895, amounted to 130l.

Meetings in February and August.

No. of Directors—6; minimum, 3; quorum, 3. Qualification, 500l.

DIRECTORS:

Chairman—W. BAILEY HAWKINS, Esq., 39, Lombard Street, E.C.

Stephenson Robert Clarke, Esq., 4. St. Dunstan's Alley, St. Dunstan's Hill, E.C.
William Clarke, Esq., M.Inst.C.E., 45, Parliament Street, S.W.

John Robert Vaizey, Esq., Attwoods, Halstead, Essex.
Hy. John Tweedy, Esq., 3, New Square, Lincoln's Inn, W.C.

OFFICERS.—Sec., William George Bailey, 3. Throgmorton Avenue, E.C.; Gen. Man., George Copus, Halstead, Essex; Auditor, James B. Laurie, A.C.A., 2, Gresham Buildings, E.C.; Solicitors, Blyth, Dutton, Hartley, and Blyth, 112, Gresham House, E.C.

Bradshaw's *Railway Shareholders Manual* of 1896 detailing the CV & H Railway.

In 1885 a revised Colne Valley & Halstead (Arrangements) Act was passed, under the terms of which the matters on which agreement could not be reached were referred to arbitration. The provisions of the Act and the Award of the Arbitrator, Lord Bramwell, are summarised in *Appendix A*. Briefly the position as a result of the Act may be stated as thus: the Company was empowered to issue £50,000 in 5% "A" Mortgage Debentures as new money; the Creditors and various bond-holders received 4% "B" Debentures in satisfaction of their claims and £25,590 Preference Shares and £61,200 Ordinary Shares remained, on which incidentally no dividend was ever paid.

Evidently some of the new capital was used for the purchase of locomotives, two new 2–4–2 tanks being delivered by Messrs Hawthorn Leslie & Co. in 1887, followed by a third in 1894, most of the earlier engines having become inadequate for the work.

In 1887 there was correspondence with the Great Eastern Railway with a view to their taking over the working of the line under the provisions of the Great Eastern Amalgamation Act (1862), which came to nothing as the latter insisted on requiring a prohibitive sum to be expended on renewals before they would consider the matter further.

The Company now seems to have settled down to a fairly peaceful and steady existence. In 1893 a railway was proposed from Haverhill to Takeley, a station on the Great Eastern Bishop Stortford–Braintree branch, followed in 1896 by one leaving the Great Eastern main line at Elsenham and running through Thaxted to Hedingham and Haverhill. In the next year a suggested Ongar, Dunmow, & Yeldham Light Railway was considered but all these proposals came to nothing. In 1898 the Colne Valley were more directly concerned by the proposed Hedingham & Bardfield Light Railway as they were invited to undertake the working of the line if and when completed. The same year, further abortive schemes for light railways were proposed between Kelvedon and Halstead via Coggeshall and from Hedingham to Long Melford and the Central Essex Light Railway (Ongar, Dunmow and Sible Hedingham), which latter obtained successive extentions of time until as late as 1914. The Company decided to oppose them all. In 1900 a Braintree & Halstead Light Railway was proposed, but the Colne Valley gave it no support.

With the coming of Mr Elyot S. Hawkins in 1903, following the retirement of Mr Copus owing to ill health, the railway entered upon a new phase and numerous alterations and improvements in the organisation and working of the line were inaugurated. When Mr Bailey, the Secretary, retired in 1904 Mr Hawkins amalgamated the office with that of General Manager, to which was also added the post of Engineer in 1912 on the retirement of Mr Fenn, who had held this position at intervals since 1868. Mr Bailey, however, continued to act as adviser to his successor for two years at a salary of £50 per annum. Shortly after his appointment, Mr Hawkins secured a fine set of three second-hand bogie coaches which were warmly received by the public as they were a great advance on anything previosly seen on the line. The next important move was the transference of the locomotive repairing and engineering department from Haverhill to Halstead about 1908, thus centralising the whole of the administration. The year 1908 also witnessed the purchase of a new 0–6–2 tank locomotive, the largest yet owned by the company. It is not without interest to note that Mr Hawkins was also responsible for the production of the first Appendix to the Working Timetable.[1]

The Colne Valley once more reopened the question of amalgamation with Great Eastern in June 1914. In a reply dated 30th July, 1914 to their formal notice, the Great Eastern denied the validity of the notice. The Board accordingly resolved to apply to the Railway & Canal Commission to determine the difference, but the outbreak of war with Germany the following month brought the matter to a close.

The first foretaste of road motor competition came in 1914 when the National Steam Car Company commenced operations in the district. The outbreak of war quickly put a stop to this, however, but the Steam Car Company's successor, the National Omnibus & Transport Company, resumed services soon after the cessation of hostilities.

We have now virtually reached the end of the history of the Colne Valley & Halstead and the remainder of its separate existence passed uneventfully in so far as local happenings were concerned, amid the turmoil of the first war with Germany and the unsettled years that followed it. The most noticeable effect of the war was the departure of Mr Hawkins and many of the younger members of his staff on active service. Mr Hawkins eventually rejoined the line in 1919, not, however, without having been wounded; a memorial plaque in the general waiting room at Halstead station commemorates those Colne Valley men who did not return.

The immediate post-war years brought nothing but the prospect of reduced earning. In 1922, in anticipation of a substantial loss of revenue, the staff agreed to submit to a 10% cut in their earnings. Fortunately, the year proved more successful than had been expected and the Board were able to restore the cut at the end of the year. This was practically the penultimate event in its history, since under the terms of the Railways Act, 1921, the Colne Valley & Halstead Railway was included in the London & North Eastern Railway as a subsidiary company (at terms given in detail in *Appendix B*). On 1st January,

1923, therefore, the small Company, which had maintained its independence in the face of crippling financial difficulties for over sixty years, finally ceased to exist.

1 *See page 91.*

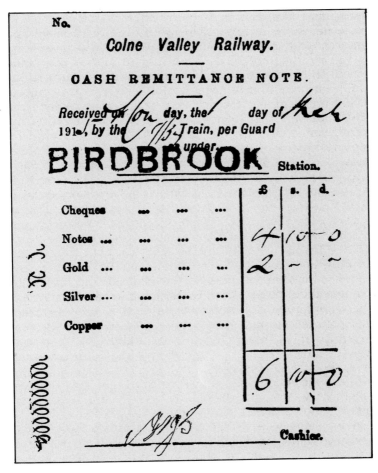

A leaf from CVR Cash Remittance book of 1915 showing that gold was still in circulation after introduction of Treasury Notes a few months earlier.

Chapter Three
Personalities

The first Chairman of the Directors of the Colne Valley and Halstead Railway was Mr Edward Hornor, of The Howe, Halstead, one of the party who met to discuss the first proposal for a railway through the Colne Valley. He was succeeded in 1860 by Mr James Brewster, who except for a brief interregnum in 1863-64 when Mr Vaughan was Chairman, retained the office until the end of 1885 and who was, as we have already noticed, extremely outspoken. No person or institution of which he did not approve would escape swift and sharp criticism uttered without fear, favour or, perhaps, the due consideration befitting a man of his status. Mr Love, the Chairman of the Eastern Counties Railway and, later, the Great Eastern Railway, particularly incurred Mr Brewster's displeasure, which is not surprising in view of the former's casual treatment of the Colne Valley. In the Directors' dispute of 1863, Mr Brewster voiced much criticism of Mr R.E. Greenwood, a fellow Director whom he accused, among other things, of securing the dismissal of the locomotive foreman for refusing to engage his (Greenwood's) son as a locomotive driver; of interfering with Mr Watt, the General Manager, and even of submitting, among his expenses, a gas bill for £7 10s. 0d. when the previous year it had amounted to only £2 10s. 0d. Others, not so outspoken, asserted that Mr Greenwood has accepted commissions on loans raised on behalf of the Company; a charge however, in support of which no evidence was adduced.[1]

On another occasion, in December 1885, Mr Brewster circulated a paper which he claimed gave "a few facts" concerning the conduct of the Company's affairs. One of the Directors, Mr Tweedy and his father, both considerable shareholders, were this time the objects of his indignation. Mr Tweedy remarked in a retaliatory letter that Mr Brewster was perfectly correct in asserting that his paper contained a few facts and added in effect that the facts were remarkably few indeed. Notwithstanding his peppery temperament, Mr Brewster commanded considerable respect in Halstead. One gathers, moreover, that he was not slow to require a reason for failure to show him the appropriate degree of diffidence. As one resident humorously put it, "If you didn't raise your hat to him, he had a mind to clap you in jail", the latter part of the remark referring to Mr Brewster's activities as a Justice of the Peace.

Mr Brewster's successor, Mr W. Bailey-Hawkins, was also abrupt in his manner at times. At the half-yearly meeting held in August 1888, Mr Jackson, a solicitor of Haverhill, was about to address the Directors on the subject of professional fees owed to him by the Colne

Valley, when the Chairman interrupted by announcing that the matter should be referred to the Company's solicitors and without more ado declared the meeting closed. The dumb-founded Mr Jackson was left standing, his speech undelivered, as the Directors dispersed.

Mr Bailey-Hawkins became seriously ill in 1919 and Mr C.B.O. Clarke occupied the Chair as his deputy during 1919 and 1920. Mr Bailey-Hawkins died in 1921 and in the same year was succeeded as Chairman by Mr Clarke who remained in office for the remainder, brief as it was, of the Colne Valley's independent existence.

Of Mr Nathaniel Beardmore, the first Engineer of the Company, little is known. His successor, Joseph Cubitt, was son of Sir William Cubitt, the prominent civil engineer of the early part of the nineteenth century, who in course of time almost outshone his father. His appointment as Engineer to the Colne Valley & Halstead Railway must be regarded largely as consultative. When one remembers that he had been Engineer to such lines as the Great Northern and the London, Chatham and Dover, the Colne Valley seems very "small fry". Cubitt probably dealt only with the broad outlines of the Colne Valley schemes, and almost all the site work was carried out by Mr C.B. Sperling, whose post was officially "sub-Engineer". However, when the line was completed throughout, the services of such a "giant" as Cubitt were no longer required and Mr Sperling became the Company's permanent Engineer, except during the brief period when the line was leased to Gooch (who, it will be remembered, appointed a Mr Rogers to manage it), and for an even briefer period during which Sperling himself was lessee.

In 1861 it would appear that Mr E.D. Cattaway fulfilled the duties of Locomotive Superintendent for the Company at 1 New Broad St. E.C., though probably in an advisory capacity only.

During the whole of its life the Company had only four Secretaries. The first, Mr Alfred Edward Williams, remained in its service for four years until Mr Edmund Harvey succeeded him in 1860. The latter held this position until December 1872, when, as a result of an alleged misappropriation of funds he was suspended and subsequently resigned. The death of Mr Harvey shortly afterwards prevented any further discussion of the charges. The next holder of the office, Mr William G. Bailey, remained with the Company until 1904 when the Secretaryship was combined with several other offices carried out by Mr Hawkins, who will be referred to again later.

The first General Manager was Mr Robert Johnston Watt. In discussing the history of the line we mentioned that Mr Watt was a far from popular character, and that "Watt-baiting" was a recognized pastime in Halstead in the 1860s. Eloquent proof of his unpopularity is afforded by the fact that when he was reappointed to this post in 1864, after the resignation of Mr Cooper, the shareholders and customers of the railway organised a protest against his return. He once had the misfortune to be sued by a Mr Goodbody of Ely[2] over some matter concerning a donkey. The wits of Halstead seized on this opportunity and to his detractors he was always "Donkey" Watt, on which nickname most of their sallies were based. There was in existence in Halstead at that time an excellent wood cut[3] of a small lop-eared donkey browsing on thistles which, by convention, was a representation of Mr Watt in his "allegorical" form. From time to time a fresh piece of "Wattiana" would issue from the presses of his detractors, each fresh effort bearing this same picture at its head. A typical example bore in addition to the donkey the following verses:

> Who when a maid in the train he spied,
> Forthwith himself set by her side?
> > MY DONKEY!
> Who when he caused a great hubbub,
> His name did quickly give as "Tubb"?
> > MY DONKEY!
> Who up and down the streets did walk,
> And on the walls did "Cooper" chalk?
> > MY DONKEY!
> Who when Gas Manager a note did bring,
> Disdainfully his hand did fling?
> > MY DONKEY!
> Who when the gallant Mac appeared,
> Called Evans out because he feared?
> > MY DONKEY!
> Who when had up before "the beak"
> Displayed a great amount of cheek?
> > MY DONKEY!
> Who now looks quite off his feed,
> His mane and tail all gone to seed?
> > MY DONKEY!
> Whose time is up? Whose race is o'er?
> Who SHALL go, as he's gone before?
> > MY DONKEY!
> > Trinity Stables.   X.B Trainer

The third and the last verse, of course, refer to the brief period in 1863–64 when Mr Cooper was Manager, but it would be interesting to know to what the other incidents and characters referred. The printer's name appeared at the bottom, "Mr Nobody, Nowhere". In another case some wag produced an imaginary balance sheet of the Company which included among the assets "The Donkey and Tubbs to feed from".

Mr Watt left the line in 1865, when it was leased to Gooch, and the *Halstead Times* noted the occasion as follows:

COLNE VALLEY RAILWAY. Many of our readers will be gratified to learn that Mr R.J. Watt, manager of the Colne Valley Railway, has obtained a lucrative appointment as Manager of the Government Railway in the island of Ceylon. The *Halstead Gazette* states "the appointment was competitive and in proof of Mr Watt's well known abilities and the high character of his credentials he was unanimously elected by the government from a large number of candidates".

We should like to be assured, as one result of the change in the management, that the long-standing accounts of tradesmen will be discharged at an early date and without that partiality of which we have heard some rumours.

It is not recorded what Mr Watt was doing during the period of the lease but at its termination he returned first as lessee himself and later as General Manager again. Presumably the appointment in Ceylon either failed to materialise or was of very short duration. He finally departed from the line in 1877, unpopular to the end, as his resignation was marked by a dispute with the Directors as to the sums due to him.

A report in the *Halstead Gazette* of 1st June, 1876 throws considerable light on the management of the line at that time, and in particular accounts for a good deal of the somewhat strained relations that existed between the Colne Valley and Great Eastern Coys.

Mr Watt, as General Manager, was chief witness for the prosecution of John Thomas Titman, the Halstead station-master, for embezzlement of the Company's monies. It soon became clear from questions by the defence and from the learned Clerk, as well as from the attitude of other witnesses, that Watt was regarded with extreme disfavour.

Watt was unable, despite every manoeuvre, to prevent the following matters coming to light. Excess fares from foreign lines were not being returned to the Railway Clearing House, the Great Eastern being the principal loser. Likewise, money so collected was not being accounted for in the Company's books. Great Eastern wagons would be loaded at Birdbrook, and invoiced as from Halstead or Colne so that mileage was lost to the owning company, and cash to the Colne Valley. Similarly Birdbrook excursion tickets were being issued from Colne with the same purpose in view.

Watt also admitted that monies received by the sale of old sleepers, ironwork and other surplus materials did not appear in the Company's books, and that timber chains off the Great Eastern were being held back and stamped CVR. It is not surprising therefore, that the Great Eastern sent two detectives to watch the proceedings.

Needless to say all the charges preferred against Titman were dismissed.

Of Mr J.B. Cooper who was Manager for a short time in 1863–64, very little is known. In June 1864, he was asked to account to the Board for alleged misconduct. However, instead of tendering any explanations he offered his resignation, which was immediately accepted and henceforth Halstead knew him no more.

Mr John Crabtree, who succeeded Watt, had been outdoor Goods Agent for the Great Northern Railway at Halifax. He left in 1882 to take up the position of General Manager of the Great Northern & Eastern Joint Railway at Lincoln, and was followed by Mr George Copus who remained General Manager until 1903, when the post was assumed by Mr Hawkins.

Mr Sperling's successor as Engineer was Mr A.G. Fenn, who joined the Colne Valley in 1868 and became Engineer in 1871. He left the Company in 1881 to join the Heberlein Brake Co. as Consulting Engineer. He returned to the Colne Valley and resumed his post as Engineer in 1903 and remained until 1912 when the position of Engineer was combined with several others.

A description of the Heberlein Brake may be of interest, especially as it is now completely obsolete. The gear was operated by a light rope which was carried on guides along the tops of the vehicles. When the train was in motion the brakes were kept in the "Off" position by a tension applied to this rope by hand reels fitted in the brake van and on the engine. A cast iron drum, cast in two halves, was bolted to one axle on each vehicle and on the engine. A wrought iron frame carried underneath the coaches supported friction rollers which were capable of being brought in and out of contact with the drum by the motion of a system of levers and rods actuated in turn by the brake rope already mentioned. The release of the tension in this rope permitted the friction rollers to come into contact with the cast iron drum which was, of course, revolving with the axle. The motion thus transmitted to the rollers was used to apply the brakes.

Colne Valley locomotive No. 1 and three passenger vehicles had this braking system experimentally installed in 1884 and a series of trials carried out on the line during that year were pronounced "very satisfactory". The brake was never used again on the Colne Valley nor, as far as the authors can trace, upon any other British railway, although it was used to some extent in South America. The defects of the system are quite obvious and were common to almost all others which attempted to solve the problem without recourse to the use of air, either under pressure or acting upon a vacuum. It had this solitary advantage over certain of the others (for example the Webb chain brake on the LNWR) that it was automatic since, if the train parted, the rope broke and released the tension which held the brake off. Apart from this it was clumsy, slow acting, incapable of proper graduation in its application and useless for long trains or high speeds. As a competitor with the Westinghouse or Vacuum brakes it was tackling hopeless odds and was, in fact, twenty years too late.

It has already been noticed that Mr Hawkins entered the service of the Colne Valley in 1903 as General Manager and subsequently became Secretary & Engineer in addition. Under Mr Hawkins' control the Company made great strides on the operating side and an extended note of his career may, therefore, be of interest. After education at Shrewsbury School, Mr Hawkins spent five years as a pupil in the shops of the Cambrian Railways at Oswestry, at the end of which he graduated to the drawing office and thence to the inspection of materials department. He finally left the Cambrain Railways in 1903 to take up his appointment on the Colne Valley.

Whilst at Oswestry he had joined the Shropshire Rifle Volunteers, which later under Lord Haldane's Territorial scheme became the 4th Battalion Kings Shropshire Light Infantry. Consequently when war broke out in 1914 he was immediately called for service with that unit with which he spent two and a half years in the Far East, in Burma, Singapore and Hong Kong. In 1917 he was transferred to the Western Front, where he remained until April 1918, when he received a wound which necessitated his repatriation. He left the Army in February 1919, with the rank of Major and returned to the Colne Valley which he continued to manage until the formation of the LNER.

An interesting personality on a humbler plane was Mr Peter Goulden who joined the Colne Valley in 1866 as Locomotive Foreman, having previously worked for the Great Western Railway at Wolverhampton. Mr Goulden had served his apprenticeship with the LNWR at Crewe and not only was he a good fitter but was capable when need arose of turning blacksmith, coppersmith or boilermaker. After serving the Company for over forty-five years he retired in 1913 and was succeeded as Foreman by Mr Charles Bartholomew, who came from the Great Eastern Railway's Stratford Works to which he returned after the absorption of the Colne Valley into the LNER.

The post of Accountant was not formally created until 1904, prior to which the duties were nominally carried out by the General Manager. When Mr Hawkins came to the line, however, he found that the work had been done for a good many years by Mr Samuel Rayner, who had joined the Colne Valley as a boy clerk and worked his way upwards, having at an intermediate stage been a Station-master. At the suggestion of Mr Hawkins, thereiore, the Directors appointed Mr Rayner Accountant, which position he filled from 1904 until his death in 1919. He was followed by Mr Scillitoe, who had also joined the Company as a boy and who had acted as Mr Rayner's Assistant during the war years when he deputised for Mr Hawkins during the latter's absence on active service.

Finally, mention must be made of Mr James Williamson, the Assistant Engineer of the Cambrian Railways, who, from 1912 until 1919 acted as Consulting Engineer to the Colne Valley. During the war years he paid frequent visits to the line to supervise those aspects of working, such as the permanent way, bridges, etc., in respect of which Mr Rayner found himself somewhat at a disadvantage owing to his lack of training in engineering.

---

[1] Doubtless the fact that Mr Greenwood was proprietor of the local Gas Works, and also Manager of the London and County Joint Stock Bank's Halstead branch did nothing to make the atmosphere less acrimonious.

[2] Before coming to Halstead he was employed by the Eastern Counties Railway at Ely as District Inspector having charge of ten stations.

[3] Reproduced below.

The Donkey which headed the scurrilous "anti-Watt" pamphlets. *Reproduced by kind permission from the original die.*

Chapter Four
The Way and Works

Although the Colne Valley & Halstead Railway, as its name would lead one to suppose, followed closely along the course of the River Colne, the route is by no means level. The line leaves the junction with the Sudbury branch at Chappel on a sharp curve and falls nearly all the way to White Colne Station after which, however, it joins the river which it then follows closely through Earls Colne to Halstead. About three-quarters of a mile beyond Earls Colne a road crosses the line on the level and a little to the east of this is the spot where the first sod was cut.

After leaving Halstead the line rises practically continuously on an average of about 1 in 300 to Sible and Castle Hedingham. The section between Hedingham and Yeldham is again almost all collar work for locomotives, but although the line still rises from Yeldham to Birdbrook, it does so by undulations. Actually the summit is a little short of Birdbrook and the track curves into that station on a down-grade of 1 in 82. The final stretch of line between Birdbrook and Haverhill North consists of a number of minor changes of gradient.

The 70 chain section between Colne Valley Junction and the junction with the Sudbury line, although strictly speaking not a part of the Colne Valley, deserves slightly extended mention as it contains the only considerable engineering works on the route of the Colne Valley trains if the Chappel viaduct, which they crossed only as an appendage to a Great Eastern train, be excepted. The line is carried over the Sturmer Road on a three arch brick viaduct, the crown of the central arch being some twenty-five feet above the road. The Great Eastern, who built the viaduct, found when they came to make the approach embankments that they had insufficient spoil available from other works in progress and were forced to dig large quantities from land acquired for the purpose in Haverhill, the resulting depression still being known locally as the "Junction Hole".

The permanant way at the time of opening consisted of 65 lbs. per yard flat-bottomed wrought iron rail, mainly in 21ft 0in. lengths secured to the wooden sleepers by dog spikes and ballasted with a two foot depth of drift gravel. In Halstead yard, however, 70 lbs. per yard rails were used. Later 75 lbs. per yard flat-bottomed rails were used, while later still a kind of cast iron chair was added with fang bolts and clips fastening the rail to the chair and sleeper. The curve away from the Great Eastern line at Chappel was relaid with bull-headed chaired track as were the points, crossings and running lines in the stations, apparently in the 1880s, the rails being 80 and 85 lbs. per yard Great Eastern pattern. When Mr Hawkins and Mr Fenn

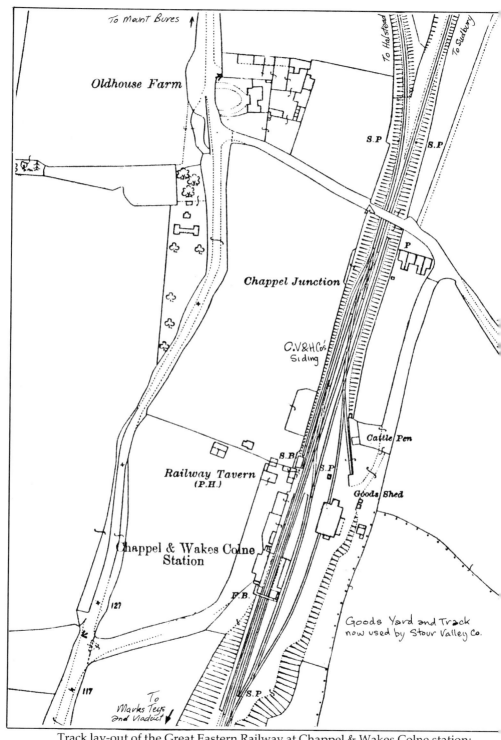

Track lay-out of the Great Eastern Railway at Chappel & Wakes Colne station:
starting point of the Colne Valley & Halstead Railway which branches *left* at
the top of the map.

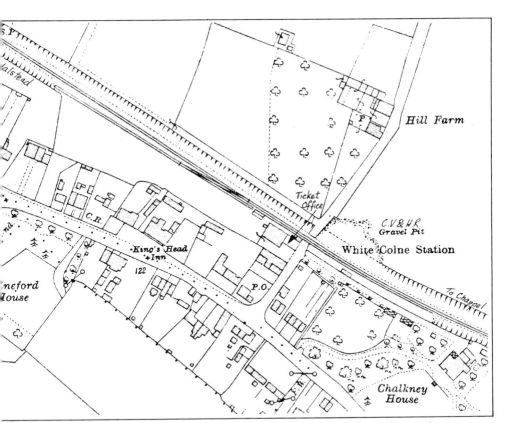

White Colne Station. Notice the platform at the opposite side of the road to the ticket office. Since this plan was made, an additional siding was laid into the spacious goods yard. The Company's ballast pit is clearly shown.

Examples of newspaper and parcel stamps.

became Manager and Engineer respectively in 1903 they found some good second-hand Great Eastern rails in stock and in 1904 these were laid between Chappel and White Colne, replacing some old 70 lbs. per yard rails. In 1913 a further length of about a mile on the Hedingham side of Halstead yard was relaid with 85 lbs. per yard bull headed rails in chairs as part of Mr Hawkins policy of replacing all the flat-bottomed track with bull-headed.

Of the original bridges, those carrying the railway over the River Colne between Chappel and Halstead were of wrought iron girders on wood piles while most of the bridges under the railway between Halstead and Haverhill consisted of cast iron girders on brick abutments. All these bridges lasted till well into the present century but the delivery of locomotive No. 5 in 1908 sounded their death-knell. Unfortunately, although Mr Hawkins had specified that this should be of the same weight as the 2–4–2 tanks it was, in fact, a little heavier and Mr Fenn was afraid to allow it to pass over the two bridges known as Whites Bridges 1 and 2 near Earls Colne station. A temporary compromise was worked out with Messrs Hudswell Clarke, the builders, whereby the coal and water capacity were temporarily decreased and in the interim a full report was made to the Board. After some persuasion the directors agreed to a full and independent inspection of *all* the bridges. As Mr W. Bailey-Hawkins, the Chairman, was also the Chairman of the Cambrian Railways (now part of the Great Western) and as Mr Hawkins had himself come from the same line, the assistance of the Chief Civil Engineer of that Company was sought. The survey was carried out by Mr James Williamson, his principal assistant, and not only completely upheld Mr Fenn's opinion concerning the Whites Bridges, but declared that the margin of safety was too small even with the 2–4–2 locomotives. He added his opinion that an early opportunity should be taken of replacing the cast iron girders on other bridges with steel. In view of the disturbing results of this survey, Mr Hawkins was given permission to carry out a programme of rebuilding or strengthening.

He began in 1908 with Whites Bridge No. 1 followed by No. 2 in 1909 and thereafter by all the other bridges requiring renewal, the last to be treated being Birdbrook Bridge in 1913. Where the entire bridge was renewed, the Colne Valley engineering staff built the new brickwork and masonry and pulled down the old structure while the Butterley Steel Company supplied and erected the new steel work. However, where the girders only were being replaced, the Colne Valley men carried out all the work, the steel being supplied by Dorman Long & Co. Ltd. ready for erection. The line was closed after the passage of the last down train on Saturday evening and the train staff handed to the engineering gang who retained it until the

The somewhat rudimentary buildings which made up Birdbrook Station seen here in the 1947 view. A train for Chappel is entering the station with 0–6–0 running tender first. The *You may telephone from here* sign seems rather odd for such a small station. *Authors' Collection*

The same station as the last view but looking towards Halstead showing signal box and well ventilated goods shed which serves the small goods yard. *Authors' Collection*

The station approach and entrance to Birdbrook Station showing clearly the original diminutive station structure. *Authors' Collection*

Yeldham Station exterior and forecourt. The original station building in the centre is flanked by later additions, with the goods shed on far right. Left of the crane are pre-fabricated structures from Whitlocks' Works on trucks, awaiting despatch. *Authors' Collection*

Yeldham Station seen from the level crossing showing another very sound signal box, the up and down starter signals and buildings. The left hand line is a siding, not part of a train crossing point. *Authors' Collection*

Yeldham Station but viewed towards Halstead, showing the loading dock and cattle pens on the right. *Authors' Collection*

The approach road and entrance to Sible and Castle Hedingham station in 1947 showing goods shed and office. Notice the interesting form of decorated brickwork. *Authors' Collection*

A 1947 view of the platform of Sible and Castle Hedingham station looking towards Halstead, showing the goods shed and signal box with a class 'J15' ex-GER 0–6–0 on a train for Haverhill. Ripper's joinery works can be seen on the right in the background. The station building has now been rebuilt (brick-by-brick) at the new Colne Valley Railway headquarters, about a mile away. *Authors' Collection*

Sible and Castle Hedingham station but looking towards Haverhill. This shows the very solid signal box and some of the staff at 1947.

Authors' Collection

An exterior view of Halstead Station showing the fencing and gate in the wall, also a loading platform and ramp (probably for milk traffic). On the left is the gate to the loading dock.

Authors' Collection

A fine period scene, undated but around 1910, showing the granary and goods shed on left (No. 3 tank engine is on shunting duty), platform and signal box in middle distance and the CV wagons and horse-box on right.

Lens of Sutton

Halstead station showing the platform, loading dock, signal box and Trinity Street crossing gates, plus a very high down home signal post. The large advertisements are of Sutton's Seeds and Crossley Oil & Gas Engines, *c*.1914.

Lens of Sutton

A 1947 view of Halstead station taken nearer to the crossing showing the loading dock and up starter on right. The advertisements have been cleared from the station wall by this time. *Authors' Collection*

A late view of Halstead looking towards Chappel, notice the alteration to the wall on left and BR pattern signs. The footbridge straddling the yard is in the distance. *Lens of Sutton*

Halstead station *c.*1885 viewed from the goods yard entry before the signal-box was moved from Parsonage Lane to Trinity Street Crossing (just off the picture left). Locomotive No. 1 is in "as received" state with some of the first 4-wheelers: a gateway and opening was made later in the platform wall near the name board. *Authors' Collection*

Former Head Office and stores of the CV & H Railway. The water softening plant, dock and passenger station can be seen in the left background. Photographed in 1947. *Authors' Collection*

passage of the up train on Sunday evening. The up and down trains on Sunday morning were worked by bringing trains up to either side of the obstruction by pilot working and allowing the passengers to walk between them. The dismantling and replacement of a bridge in less than twenty-two hours by the men of such a small line was an extremely commendable achievement.

The fact that no serious accidents occured on the line during the first twenty-five years of its operation can hardly be attributed to an elaborate system of signalling. In fact it is probable that for the first twelve months or so the Company worked their traffic on the "one engine in steam" principle. However, by 1863 at the latest, the electric telegraph was installed, for in May of that year Sanger's Circus visited Halstead and, so the *Halstead Gazette* informs us, was impeded in its passage over the Trinity Street level crossing by the low telegraph wires. There is evidence that only partial interlocking of points and signals was in use on the lines under the sole control of the Colne Valley until the passing of the Regulation of Railways Act, 1889. The work entailed under that Act, which enforced the interlocking of points and signals and the use of continuous automatic brakes on passenger trains, necessitated an increase of £12,150 in the Loans and Debenture Stock, the necessary authority being obtained by an Order of the Board of Trade under the powers conferred upon it by the Act.

Latterly the line was divided into six sections for purposes of single line working. Between Chappel and Colne the trains were controlled by the electric train staff, but on the remaining sections to the Colne Valley station at Haverhill the train staff and ticket system was in use.

The original staff section extended the whole way from Chappel to Halstead but, probably as a result of pressure from the Great Eastern, the section from Chappel to Earls Colne had been converted to the electric train staff. However, when Mr Hawkins took over, he found the old staff with its markings for Chappel still in use between Earls Colne and Halstead but no box for tickets at Earls Colne, the ticket book being loose on the counter. Temporary arrangements were immediately made to ensure safety until the box could be repaired, but soon afterwards the new Manager discovered a complete set of new boxes and staff still in the manufacturer's wrapping in the stores at Halstead where they had languished since the sections had been rearranged.

The signals were controlled from seven signal boxes, viz.: Earls Colne, Halstead–Parsons (or Parsonage) Lane,[1] Halstead–Trinity Street, Castle Hedingham, Yeldham and Colne Valley Junction, and Great Eastern Railway's Chappel box. In addition there were signal frames at Fox & Pheasant Crossing (between Chappel and White

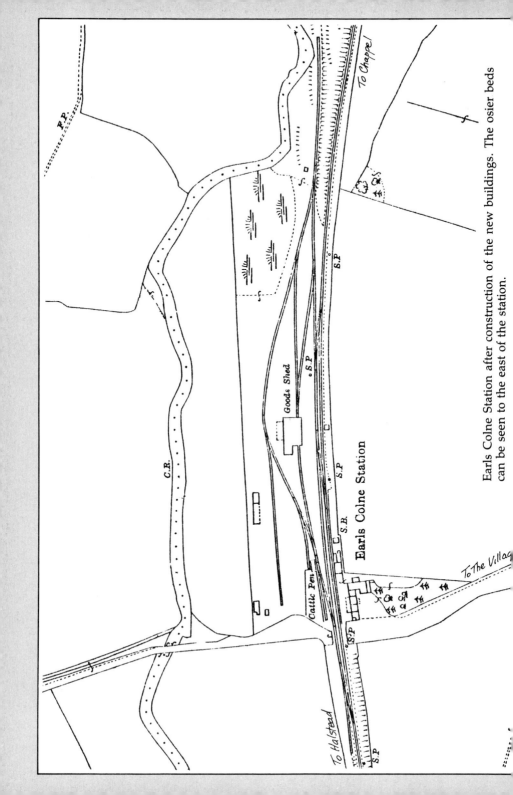

Earls Colne Station after construction of the new buildings. The osier beds can be seen to the east of the station.

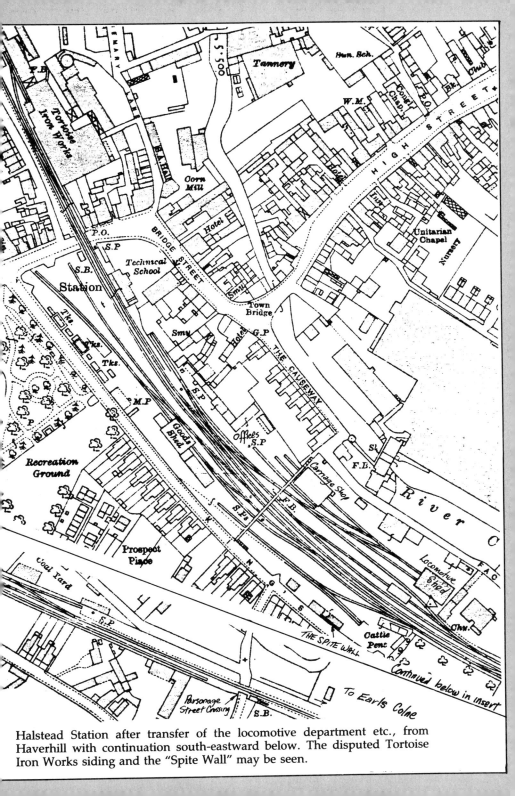

Halstead Station after transfer of the locomotive department etc., from Haverhill with continuation south-eastward below. The disputed Tortoise Iron Works siding and the "Spite Wall" may be seen.

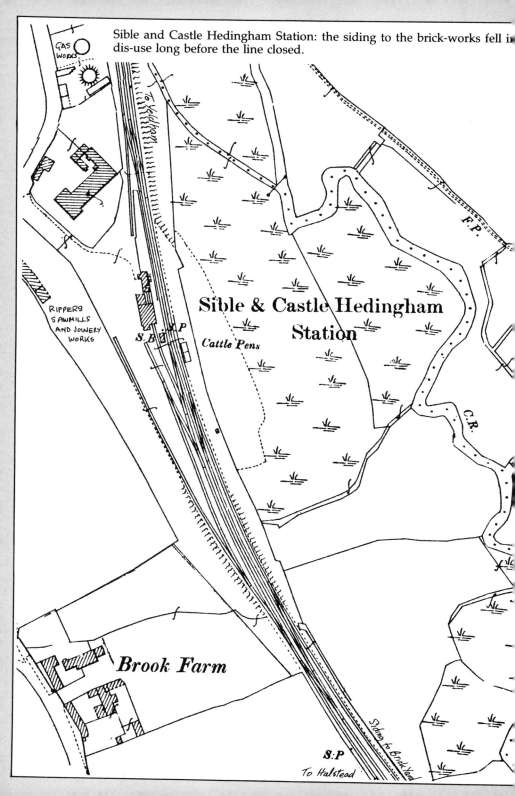

Sible and Castle Hedingham Station: the siding to the brick-works fell in dis-use long before the line closed.

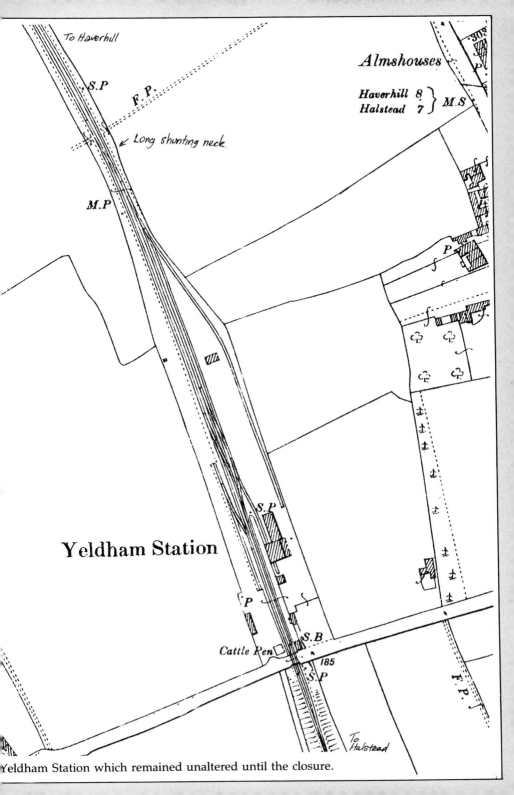

To Haverhill

S.P

F.P.

Long shunting neck.

M.P

Almshouses

Haverhill 8 }
Halstead 7 } M.S

P

P

P

Yeldham Station

S.P

P

Cattle Pen

S.B

185

S.P

F.P.

To Halstead

Yeldham Station which remained unaltered until the closure.

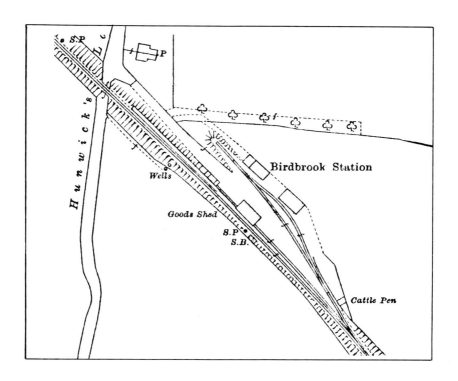

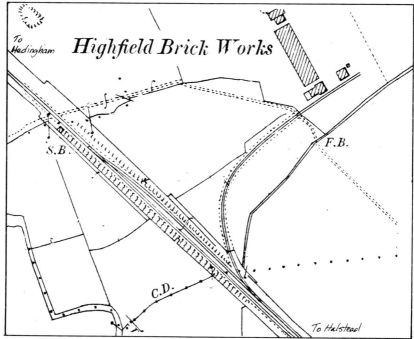

Above: Birdbrook Station, at date not known the north siding became a dead-end, the loop connection having been taken out.

Below: Purls Hill Siding. Note the passing loop (taken out later) for working the traffic to and from Highfield Brick Works.

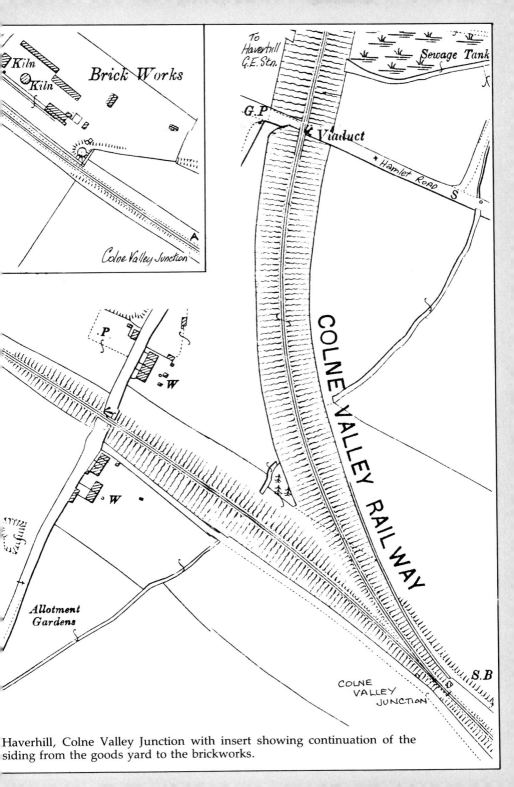

Haverhill, Colne Valley Junction with insert showing continuation of the siding from the goods yard to the brickworks.

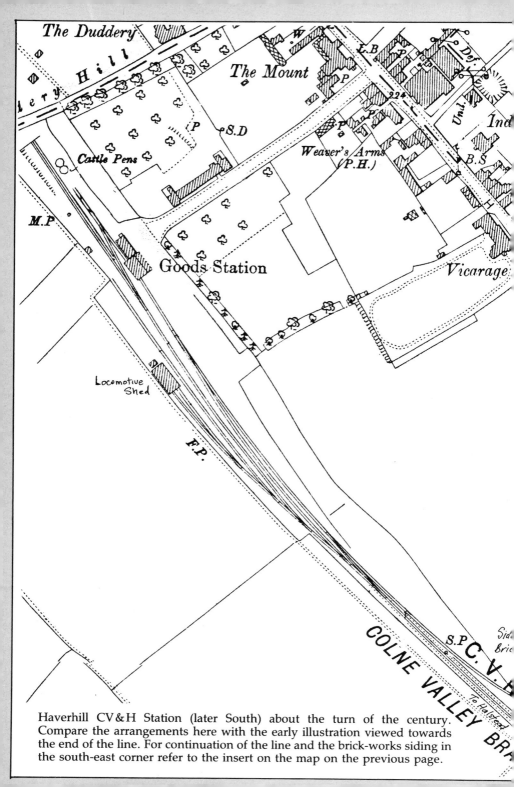

The Duddery

ery Hill

The Mount

W

L.B

Def.

Ind.

P

224

Unl.

P

S.D

P

P

Weaver's Arms
(P.H.)

B.S

Cattle Pens

M.P

Goods Station

Vicarage

Locomotive
Shed

F.P.

S.P.

C. V. H

COLNE VALLEY BR

To Halstead

Sid
bric

Haverhill CV&H Station (later South) about the turn of the century.
Compare the arrangements here with the early illustration viewed towards
the end of the line. For continuation of the line and the brick-works siding in
the south-east corner refer to the insert on the map on the previous page.

Remains of original Earls Colne station of 1860 just prior to demolition in 1905, with part of the new station in the background. The board over the door proclaims George Evans Collector. The advertisements are interesting and Wenley's are still in business as Bolingbroke & Wenley in Chelmsford.

Authors' Collection

Earls Colne station showing the exterior of the new station and station house, which would be a credit to any major railway. A Thornycroft local delivery lorry of the LNER is on the left. *Authors' Collection*

Earls Colne station in 1954 looking towards Halstead showing the signal box and crossing gates, the goods yard was on the right. *Lens of Sutton*

The same station seen in 1947 from the level crossing, the small enclosure under the canopy was the ladies' waiting room. *Authors' Collection*

The frontal aspect of the platform at Earls Colne station when new. The left hand doors gave access to the booking office; first class waiting room was on the right and the porters' room and gentlemen further right.

Authors' Collection

Another view of Earls Colne station (from an old postcard) showing the goods shed and associated buildings.   *Lens of Sutton*

The first Whites Bridge built on timber piers over the River Colne, for the opening in 1860 ; replaced 1909. *Authors' Collection*

The replacement Whites Bridge of 1909, a thoroughly workmanlike piece of engineering. *Authors' Collection*

White Colne station viewed towards Halstead. The small brick cabin for the crossing-keeper is now at the Hedingham headquarters of the new CVR Company. The booking office was reached through the white porch, with the goods yard behind the house. *Authors' Collection*

White Colne station in 1947 with the house and cabin on right. The platform is beyond the crossing gates. *Authors' Collection*

A 1954 view of White Colne station. The waiting room is the body off an early 4-wheeler and the lock-up, a former box van. *Lens of Sutton*

Another view of White Colne taken from a train window. 1956. *H. Casserley*

An Up train approaching the junction at Chappel and Wakes Colne station.
H. Casserley

The exterior of GER Chappel and Wakes Colne station in 1947 with its unusual staircase entrance. The original station buildings lay beyond, entered from a gate by the white villa: the up platform is visible behind the footbridge. A fine building for a small rural station. *Authors' Collection*

The same station viewed, facing Marks Tey. The up platform is on the left
with the parapet wall of Colne Valley Viaduct just visible. These buildings
and the footbridge have since been removed.   *Authors' Collection*

Looking towards Sudbury, the CV&H Railway siding is on left between
signal box and the overline bridge (note the splendid goods shed on right).
The footbridge has lost its roofing and the outside stairs can be seen left.
                                                     Authors' Collection

CV&H Railway stations and mileage included in table below.

GREAT EASTERN RAILWAY

Stations in Essex, with number of Miles from London.

		COLCHESTER LINE.	
	¼	Bishopsgate	
	1¼	Bethnal Green (Junction)	
	1¾	Globe road and Devonshire Street	
	2¼	Coborn-road	
	4	Stratford (Junction)	
	4½	Maryland Point	
	5¼	Forest Gate (Junction)	
	6¼	Manor Park	
	7½	Ilford	
	8¼	Seven Kings	
	9¼	Goodmayes	
	10	Chadwell Heath	
	12	Romford	
	15	Harold Wood	
	18¼	Brentwood and Warley	
	20¼	Shenfield and Hutton (Junction)	
	24½	Billericay	
	29¼	Wickford (Junction)	
	31¾	Battles Bridge	
	34¼	Woodham Ferris (Junction)	
	37½	Cold Norton	
	41½	Maldon (West)	
	42¾	Maldon (East)	
	37½	Fambridge	
	40½	Althorne	
	43½	Burnham-on-Crouch	
	45¾	Southminster	
	33¼	Rayleigh	
	36¼	Hockley	
	38¾	Rochford	
	41	Prittlewell	
	41½	Southend-on-Sea	
	23½	Ingatestone	
	29¾	Chelmsford	
	36	Hatfield Peverel	
	38¼	Witham (Junction)	
	44	Maldon	
	44½	Braintree	
	41¾	Kelvedon	
	46¼	Marks Tey (Junction)	
	49¾	Chappel (Junction for Bures)	
CV&H	52½	Colne	
CV&H	56½	Halstead	
CV&H	59½	Castle Hedingham	
CV&H	62½	Yeldham	
CV&H	66½	Birdbrook	
CV&H	69½	Haverhill	
	55¼	Bures	
	58½	Sudbury	
	51¼	Colchester (Junction)	
	53½	St. Botolph's	
	55	Hythe	
	57¼	Wyvenhoe	
	62½	Brightlingsea	
	58¾	Alresford	
	60½	Thorrington	
	61¾	Bentley Green	
	63¾	Weeley	
	65¾	Thorpe (Junction)	
	71	Clacton-on-Sea	
	68½	Kirby Cross	
	71	Walton-on-the-Naze	
	55½	Ardleigh	
	59	Manningtree (Junction)	
	60¾	Mistley	
	62	Bradfield	
	64½	Wrabness	
	68¼	Parkeston Quay	
	69¼	Dovercourt	
	69¾	Harwich	
		CAMBRIDGE LINE.	
	22	Roydon	
	24¾	Burnt Mill	
	26¼	Harlow	
	28½	Sawbridgeworth	
	32¼	Bishop's Stortford (Junction)	18
	37½	Takeley (miles from Braintree	12¾
	34	Easton ,,	10½
	31¾	Dunmow ,,	8½
	44	Felsted ,,	6¼
	48	Rayne ,,	2¼
	35¼	Stansted	
	37½	Elsenham	
	41¾	Newport	
	43½	Audley End (Junction)	
	45½	Saffron Walden	
	78¾	Haverhill	
	47½	Great Chesterford	
		ILFORD TO WOODFORD LOOP LINE.	
		Ilford	
		Newbury Park ½ miles from Ilfd.	
		Barkingside 1 ,, ,,	
		Fairlop 2 ,, ,,	
		Hainault 2½ ,, ,,	
		Grange Hill 3 ,, ,,	
		Chigwell 3½ ,, ,,	
		Woodford 4½ ,, ,,	
		ONGAR BRANCH.	
	5½	Leyton	
	6½	Leytonstone	
	7½	Snaresbrook	
	8¼	George Lane	
	9½	Woodford	
	10¾	Buckhurst Hill	
	12	Loughton	
	13½	Chigwell Lane	
	15½	Theydon Bois	
	17	Epping	
	19½	North Weald	
	21½	Blake Hall	
	23½	Ongar	
		WOOLWICH BRANCH.	
	4½	Stratford Market	
	6	Canning Town, for Barking Road	
	7¼	Victoria Docks	
	8	Silvertown	
	9	North Woolwich	
		CHINGFORD LINE.	
		Liverpool Street	
	5¾	St. James' Street, Walthamstow	
	6½	Hoe Street ,,	
	7½	Wood Street ,,	
	8¾	Hale End	
	10	Chingford	
		KELVEDON TO TOLLESBURY LIGHT RAILWAY.	
		Kelvedon	
		Tiptree	3 miles from Kelvedon
		Tolleshunt D'Arcy	6 ,,
		Tollesbury	9

In the above tabulation Chappel station is shown as Junction for Bures, this is a mistake, for Bures is the next station towards Sudbury on the GE line: it should read "Junction for Colne Valley line". *The Essex Almanac, 1905*

Colne), White Colne and Birdbrook. The points of the Halstead Coal Yard Sidings, Castle Hedingham Station Yard, Yeldham Shunting Yard and Purls Hill Brick Yard siding were controlled by Annetts Key, in the case of Purls Hill Siding the key being attached to the train staff.

Between Colne Valley Junction and Haverhill Great Eastern Junction, the Great Eastern Railway was in charge of the signalling, the block telegraph and train staff and ticket being used. In Great Eastern days, there was another signal box known as Haverhill Station Box situated close to the underline bridge at the western end of the station up platform. This has since been removed, and all signalling and movements controlled from the Junction Box. The short stretch of 16 chains between the two Haverhill boxes was worked as double-line Block. The original box at Colne Valley junction was almost square on plan and had a pavilion roof, while the actual signal posts protruded above the eaves, the two posts being joined by a kind of verandah spanning the roof. The signals were of an old-fashioned pattern, each post bearing two semaphore arms, one on either side, a single lamp thus sufficing for two signals.

An extremely amusing account of this box is contained in the *Railway Magazine* for December 1906, which comments on the arrangements as follows:

> The most curious thing . . . is the position of the signals controlling the junction. It will be seen that they are placed almost exactly level with the points. Thus, if a train were to come along the branch . . . leading from Haverhill station (Great Eastern Railway) and one were also to approach along . . . the line leading from the Colne Valley & Halstead station, the two would collide before reaching the signals. To avoid this, instructions have been issued that engines are not to foul the junction except when the proper signalls are "off". Another possibility is that two trains could meet on the single line face to face, touching, without going past a signal at danger. To complete a description of this 20th century junction it may be mentioned that the line, which is single, has no "block" instruments, the only intimation that the signal-man receives that a train is coming is by the ordinary telegraph instrument.

Its successor, the present box, although probably more efficient, is not of such arresting design.

The stations generally are the originals except in the case of Earls Colne which was opened later than the others and has been rebuilt since. At Chappel & Wakes Colne the Great Eastern station was used although the Colne Valley owned a strip of land beside the down line north of the station upon which they had a siding. Originally, this extended right up to the level crossing giving access to the goods yard, but upon the Great Eastern rebuilding the station, they erected the present signal box together with a platelayer's hut on this land. This action was always a sore point with the Colne Valley. The smallest station is White Colne which consists merely of a siding and yard adjoining a level crossing, with a single storey cottage serving as booking, parcels and goods office and gatekeeper's house in one, and a short platform with the body of an old four-wheeled coach as a waiting room. It is a little curious, however, in that the intending passenger must take his ticket at the cottage and then cross the public road to gain access to the platform. White Colne was originally known as Colne but sometime after the opening of Ford Gate station in 1882 the name was transferred to the new station, the older station being closed to traffic. However, it was reopened for goods in 1907 under its present name and passenger traffic was resumed the following year.

The present Earls Colne station was known originally as Ford Gate but the name was changed later to Colne. The buildings first erected, however, were neither handsome nor commodious – to borrow the favourite epithets of the period – consisting solely of the shed which may be clearly seen in one of the illustrations. The wooden erection near the signal box – which serves as a Ladies' Waiting Room – together with the verandah was put up during Mr Copus's regime, and went a little way towards improving the very inadequate accommodation.

In 1903 Mr Hunt, of Earls Colne, the traffic to and from whose engineering works formed a substantial part of the goods handled at the station, offered to give to the Colne Valley & Halstead Railway the necesary land for an enlarged station and to advance such sums as were required at 4% interest. The present buildings were, therefore, erected, their handsome appearance being well illustrated by the photographs. The opportunity was taken in 1905 to change the name of the station to Earls Colne in order to avoid confusion with Colne in Lancashire.

It has already been noticed in *Chapter 1* that Halstead station is that constructed shortly after the opening, with the exception of the platform canopy, which was reconstructed in 1914. The fine goods shed and the former general offices and other buildings are, however, substantial red brick structures with slated roofs and were erected during the reconstruction of the arrangements carried out during the latter days of Mr Copus's regime. The track layout plan gives a good idea of the spacious way in which the yard has been arranged. The water supply for the locomotives was drawn from a deep well just in front of the Station-master's office. Although this provided a very reliable supply, the hardness of the water detracted somewhat from its usefulness. It was eventually decided to erect a water softener, and a plant was ordered from Messrs Lassen & Hjort, the erection being completed in 1916. Its effective life was comparatively short since the use of Halstead as a locomotive depot came to an end after the grouping, and it was thus rendered more or less redundant although still in existence. It will be noticed that there is a level crossing at each end of the yard, one of which carries the road to Braintree and Gosfield across the railway. Although inconvenience is often caused both to the railway and to road users by the crossing, it would be a difficult matter to overcome.

At Sible & Castle Hedingham the station building is a simple brick structure with a wooden goods shed adjoining. The remains of what appears to be a platform on the north side of the line is the site of the former cattle pens, near to which was a carriage shed of which no trace remains. The extensive sawmill and joinery works of Messrs Ripper Bros. is situated on the south side of the yard, while a long siding leaves the line on the opposite side, crosses the River Colne and enters a brickyard. The siding is now derelict and the river bridge which is partly of wood and partly of cast iron girders is in a precarious state.

At Yeldham station again the buildings are mainly of brick but there is in addition a water tower and a brick pump-house housing a motor driven pump. The Office consists of a small corrugated iron and timber hut. This, together with a similar erection at Birdbrook station were put up in 1907. The works of Messrs Whitlock Bros, manufacturers of agricultural wagons and carts, adjoin the railway yard.

Excepting only White Colne, Birdbrook, which was opened in 1863, is the simplest station on the line, and the accommodation consists only of a small brick building for the waiting room and an office standing apart. There is a small goods shed and a privately owned grain store in the yard.[2]

Birdbrook really represents the last Colne Valley passenger station as even in pre-group days practically no trains used Haverhill South. Since then even the somewhat rudimentary arrangements provided for passengers at the latter have disappeared and all that remains is the grass covered mound where the platform formerly stood. The goods shed is still in use, together with the small locomotive shed, somewhat less substantially constructed of timber and corrugated iron, with a roof of asbestos sheeting, which in 1915, replaced the shed built in 1862 when the Company established its first locomotive depot at Haverhill shortly after the line reached that town.[3] No details appear to have survived of the equipment installed at that time but it is probable that it was of extremely meagre description and that none but the simplest repairs were carried out there. It seems that in the early days repairs were sometimes carried out by contractors since the placing of such contracts was one of the points of attack upon Mr R.E. Greenwood, an early Director, who was unfortunate enough to incur the displeasure of some of his fellow members of the Board. Mr Greenwood, it appears, either owned or had an interest in an engineering works, and was alleged to have used his influence to secure the placing of repair contracts to his own advantage. While the question of the justice or otherwise of these allegations is of little moment here, it seems safe to draw the inference that the practice of "farming out" repairs was an established fact at the time they were made. Later on, when the relationship of the Colne Valley and the Great Eastern had become more amicable major repairs were almost always turned over to the latter's works at Stratford.

From the Colne Valley's point of view this system had more than one defect. The locomotives were not sufficiently numerous to carry on the service unaided while one of them was absent at Stratford and recourse had to be made to hiring from the Great Eastern; quite apart from which the actual repairs cost more than they would have done had they been carried out in the Colne Valley's own shop. Despite its drawbacks this procedure continued until well into the present century and was brought to an end only on the appointment of Mr Hawkins as General Manager.

Mr Hawkins' first action to remedy the trouble was the removal in 1905 of the locomotive shop from Haverhill to Halstead. The equipment in the new shop, although modest, was much more satisfactory than that in the original works at Haverhill. There was an overhead travelling gantry carrying two sets of 12 ton pulley blocks and a second one provided with one set of 2 ton and one set of 3 ton Weston differential pulley blocks. The machines comprised a treadle lathe, a hand screwing machine, a port facing machine, and a hand drilling machine. There was, in addition a Smith's shop equipped with two forges and an outside Smith's shop with a pair of hand rolls for rolling plates. Needless to say, wheel turning or work of that type still had to be sent to outside works, but the sending away of one part for machining was a vastly more economical proposition than the despatch of a complete locomotive.

This alteration in the repair facilities, coupled with the purchase of the new 0–6–2 locomotive No. 5 in 1908, placed Mr Hawkins in the position which he had set out to achieve, namely, of making the Colne Valley locomotive department capable of standing on its own feet. It is a fact that only once did motive power need to be hired after this. On this occasion the heavy gantry was in use for the repair of one of the engines, when another unfortunately happened to shear a coupling rod pin, necessitating lifting to enable the repair to be dealt with – the only course open was to send the locomotive to Stratford, and to hire from Great Eastern during its absence.

The carriage and wagon shop was also at Halstead and was sufficiently equipped to carry out most repairs, although no wagon building was ever attempted. Another interesting sideline carried on at Halstead was the manufacture of tarpaulin sheets. The Company did not, of course, use an enormous number during a year but repairing existing sheets provided sufficient work to keep one man fully occupied and sometimes two.

---

[1] The original Parsonage Lane box was destroyed in the accident of 1899 and it was replaced by a tall brick box 25 ft 0 in. high to the deck. There were, however, only four levers in it controlling the signals protecting the gates. The gates themselves were hand operated and the climbing and descending of the steps was a great hardship to the gatekeeper who had lost an arm. Hawkins removed the levers to the lower half, which would have held the locking gear had there been any, and constructed an earth ramp up to it. This "white elephant" is now derelict and a ground frame is used instead.

[2] One important task attaching to the staff duties at Birdbrook Station was the collection and cancellation of all Haverhill tickets.

[3] It seems (according to the *Colchester Gazette*) that there was a little difficulty about getting the last section of the line opened because no turntable was provided at Haverhill. It is not clear whether it was the Great Eastern or Col. Yolland, the Board of Trade Inspector, who wanted it, or whether it was to be sited at Haverhill South or the Great Eastern; but the Colne Valley was to pay for it!

Chapter Five

Locomotives, Rolling Stock and Other Matters

The locomotive history of the Colne Valley & Halstead Railway begins while the line was yet under construction, the contractor's locomotives being two small 2–4–0 tank engines built by George England & Co., of Hatcham Ironworks, London. For a short time they were used by Mr Munro to work the normal traffic of the line after the opening, he having been granted a lease for this purpose as noted in *Chapter 1*. They were very soon required for work on the construction of the remainder of the line, however, and the Company had to make other arrangements. They were very neat little machines with outside cylinders, side tanks, inside frames and bearings, and with feed pumps driven off the cross-heads. The coal bunker was very small and a traversing-jack was carried. Their names were *Cam* and *Colne* and they had 11 in. x 13 in. cylinders and driving wheels about 3 ft 8 in. in diameter. The remaining dimensions have not survived and must be left to surmise, therefore, although it is highly probable that they were two of the small contractor's locomotives that George England and Co. used to build for stock in the 1850s. The late Mr Alfred Rosling Bennet wrote of how, in his boyhood, he used to climb on to the window sills of the erecting shop at Hatcham Ironworks where it fronted on Pomeroy Street and peer through the windows at the line of small blue engines offered for sale. The *Cam* had the misfortune to be involved in a fire in the shed at Haverhill but the damage proved to be capable of repair and both engines survived to do duty on other contracts, being subsequently employed on the construction of the Brightlingsea Railway (opened in 1866) and in County Clare where they probably assisted in the construction of the Athenry and Ennis Railway, which was opened in 1869.

The two locomotives which took their place on the Colne Valley early in 1861 were both purchased second-hand. One was a 2–4–0 tender locomotive from the Eastern Counties Railway and the other was an elderly 2–2–2 well tank from the London, Brighton & South Coast Railway. The former was alleged to be a product of the Leeds firm of Kitson, Thompson and Hewitson from whose shops it appeared reputedly in 1845 bearing the works number 32. It is doubtful, however, if this is correct, for Colonel E. Kitson Clark tells us in his book *Kitsons of Leeds* that the Kitson, Thompson & Hewitson partnership began in 1843 and that the locomotives they turned out were given the works numbers 37 to 649. This would seem to place the origin of the locomotive in the preceding Laird and Kitson era in 1841. The engine is further reputed to have been built for the Midland Railway and this would accord with its being constructed in 1842, since in that year Laird and Kitson supplied two "long boiler" 2–4–0s

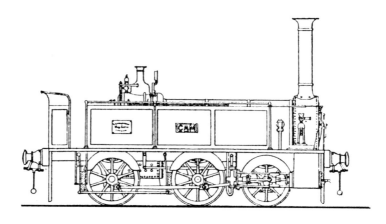

The early 2–4–0T locomotive *Cam* which was hired from Mr Munro the contractor. *Colne* was a similar engine. *Courtesy The Locomotive Magazine*

The 2–4–0 tender locomotive purchased second-hand from the Eastern Counties Railway. *Courtesy The Locomotive Magazine*

to the Midland. It was purchased by Eastern Counties Railway in 1847, becoming their No. 140. On the absorption of the Norfolk Railway locomotives into the Eastern Counties stock in 1849 an extensive renumbering took place when its number was changed from 140 to 217. The locomotive was later still renumbered 95, probably in 1856 when a batch of Gooch 2–4–0 locomotives (the "Butterflies"), delivered to the Eastern Counties from the Canada Works, Birkenhead, were allocated the numbers 215–219. The details that have survived of the dimensions are very incomplete. They are: cylinders 14 in. x 18 in.; leading wheels 3 ft 0 in. diameter and driving wheels 4 ft 6 in. diameter. The engine had a four-wheeled tender, inside frames and cylinders, a domed firebox and inclined spring bolts, and was painted green.

Details of the ex-London, Brighton & South Coast Railway locomotive are given by C.F. Dendy-Marshall in his *History of the Southern Railway*. It was originally LBSCR No. 50, later renumbered 45 and was, in the first instance, part of the rolling stock of the Joint Committee which managed the locomotives and vehicles used on the London & Croydon Railway in whose list it bore the number 88. It passed to the LBSCR under the terms of division of the London & Croydon rolling stock consequent upon the dissolution of the Joint Committee on 31st January, 1846. the builders were Sharp Roberts & Co., and the locomotive was one of their 2–2-2 express type which they supplied, with slight modifications, to a number of lines. The *History of the Southern Railway*[1] gives the building date as 1844 and the dimensions as: cylinders 15 in. x 18 in. and driving wheels 5 ft 6 in. diameter. Correlating this with Burtt's *Locomotives of the London, Brighton & South Coast Railway* this would mean, by a little deduction that it was works number 275. Burtt also gives the building date as November 1844 which accords with the information given by Dendy Marshall. Unfortunately Burtt made one of his rare mistakes in connection with this locomotive and on a later page he contradicts himself by giving an incorrect works number for the same engine. This confusion on his part is most unfortunate for it means that it is not possible to trace in detail its career on the Brighton Railway nor to give with certainty any further dimensions.

The locomotive was curious in that it had no brake gear on the left hand side, the only brake blocks provided being one on the driving and one on the trailing wheels on the right hand side. It was involved in an accident on Wednesday 10th October, 1855, near Spa Road Junction when it was bringing a train of empty carriages into London Bridge from the depot at New Cross. By mistake the points were set so that it entered a siding. Possibly because of the primitive braking system the driver was unable to stop it in time and after demolishing a wall at the end of the siding it fell into College Street below, the carriages piling up on top of it. The crew had the presence of mind to jump clear when they saw what was happening. The locomotive was not as badly damaged as might have been expected. The driver, Mr C. Taunton, continued to drive the engine after it had been repaired and he went with it to the Colne Valley & Halstead Railway on which he worked until his death at Haverhill a few years later. In its latter days on the Brighton Railway it was rebuilt as a tank engine by removing the tender and substituting a bunker; a small well tank under the cylinders; and a somewhat larger one under the footplate. It would appear that in either this rebuilding or the repairs after its accident, it received new cylinders, wheels and cranks since the dimensions quoted in the *Locomotive Magazine* for 15th June, 1911 are as follows:

> Wheels, driving ....6 ft 6 in.
> Cylinders ....15 in. x 22 in.

Later, when the engine was offered for sale, the advertisement in the *Railway Times* of 16th January, 1861 gives the wheel diameter as 5 ft 6 in. from which it will be realised that it is extremely difficult to be dogmatic about the dimensions of this locomotive. Close inspection of the illustration will show that alterations to the sizes of the wheels have taken place. The colour scheme of this locomotive was brown for the framing and green for the remainder.

It has not been possible to ascertain precisely how long these two veterans remained in service or their ultimate fate but they cannot have been used for more than a few years since they were both almost worn out when purchased. Their duties were taken over by a set of three 2–4–0 well tank engines built to the order of Mr Charles Brewster, of Little Maplestead and loaned by him to the Colne Valley. They were named *Brewster, Colne* and *Halstead* respectively and were products of Messrs Manning, Wardle & Co., from whose shops they issued in 1861, 1862 and 1863 bearing the works numbers 34, 59 and 61. *Brewster* had weatherboards only, but the later engines were fitted with cabs. The engines had 14 in. x 18 in. outside cylinders, 5 ft 0 in. diameter drivers and 3 ft 9 in. diameter leading wheels, the total wheel-base being 14 ft 0 in. The boiler had a total heating surface of 720 sq. ft., made up of 66 sq. ft firebox and 654 sq. ft tubes and the grate area was 9.5 sq. ft. The tanks when full held 490 gallons. These engines worked until 1887, when, owing to the traffic having become to heavy for them, they were dispaced by fresh engines. *Brewster* and *Halstead* were broken up at Haverhill but *Colne* was kept for a while as a spare engine and was finally sold to a colliery near Wigan. Throughout their existence they had no numbers and were referred to in the official records only by name. Their livery was, at first, dark green but this was latterly changed to brown.

No further locomotives were purchased until 1876, when, as was noticed in the preceding paragraph, the traffic began to outgrow the capacity of the Manning, Wardle engines. Accordingly an order was placed with Neilson & Co., of Glasgow, for an 0–4–2 side-tank engine. This was virtually the same design as Mr S.W. Johnson's 81 (or T7) class of the Great Eastern Railway which had appeared in 1870 and the last of which was withdrawn in 1907. It was delivered to the Colne Valley in 1877 (Works No. 2204) and the dimensions were:

Cylinders ....15in. x 22in.
Coupled wheels ....5ft 3in. diameter
Trailing wheels ....3ft 7in. diameter
Total wheelbase ....14ft 6in.
Heating surface:
    Tubes ....680.3 sq. ft
    Firebox .... 72.3 sq. ft

    Total ....752.6 sq. ft
    Grate Area ....12.7 sq.ft

The engine was twice rebuilt during its long career, the first time by Messrs Hawthorn Leslie & Co., of Newcastle-on-Tyne who added two supplementary tanks over the front splashers and modified the cab. At the same time it was painted a dark red. In 1894 it was rebuilt again, this time by the Great Eastern Railway at Stratford Works, when it acquired a stove pipe chimney, and, incidentally, a coat of black paint. Some fifteen years later, however, it reverted to a bell topped chimney when some repairs were being carried out at Halstead, the supplementary water tanks being removed at the same time. This engine survived to be taken over by the London and North Eastern Railway. The engine was always known as number 1 on the Colne Valley although it is by no means certain that the number was always painted on it.

The next addition to the locomotive stock, a second-hand purchase, was made in 1878 or 1879 shortly after Mr Crabtree's appointment as General Manager, with the intention of obviating some of the hirings from the Great Eastern Railway which were becoming increasingly frequent. The new engine was one of eighteen 0–6–0 tank engines supplied to the Cornwall Minerals Railway in 1873–4 by Messrs Sharp Stewart and Co., to the designs of Mr Francis Trevithick. They were intended to work in pairs coupled footplate to footplate and were arranged accordingly. When the Great Western Railway took over the Cornwall Minerals Railway in 1877 they sold nine of the engines back to the makers, who disposed of them as the opportunity arose. The engine acquired by the Colne Valley & Halstead Railway bore the Cornwall Minerals Railway number 10 (Works number 2358) which it retained for a time. Subsequently this was removed and a nameplate bearing the name *Haverhill* was substituted while at the same time the engine was repainted green. Early in its career on the Colne Valley a weatherboard was added at the rear of the cab to make it habitable when the engine was running bunker first. The dimensions were:

```
Cylinders .........................16¼in x 20in.
Wheels ...........................3ft 6in.
Heating surface:
  Tubes ..........................752.8 sq. ft
  Firebox ........................ 70.7 sq. ft

  Total ..........................823.5 sq. ft
Grate Area ......................10.8 sq. ft
Pressure ........................140 lbs per sq. in.
Weight in working order .........30 tons 16 cwt
```

The locomotive worked on the Colne Valley until 1889 but never received a number. Eventually it was sold to the South Hetton Colliery, Co. Durham, part of the property of South Hetton & Murton Coal Co., and continued to give yeoman service as their No. 21 with the name *Haverhill* on the tanksides on the brass nameplates fixed by the Colne Valley until 1948. Its duties consisted of three shifts daily entailing continuous work from 3 am on Mondays to 1 pm on Saturdays. The nameplates are preserved in the Headquarters of the Stephenson Locomotive Society.

A further second-hand locomotive was bought in 1883 from the Whitehaven Colliery Company. It originated in 1860 as one of five 0−4−2 inside cylinder saddle tank engines built for the North London Railway by Beyer, Peacock & Co. (Works No. 190) and bore the North London Railway number 42. The trailing wheels were carried on a radial axle of the type then popular with the North London Railway and a screw reverser was fitted. A hand-brake was fitted working on to wooden brake blocks fitted to the coupled wheels. The leading dimensions were:

```
Cylinders .........................16in. x 24in.
Coupled wheels ...................5ft 0in. diameter
Trailing wheels ..................3ft 6in. diameter
Total wheelbase ..................14ft 2in.
```

Heating surface:
Tubes ....857 sq. ft
Firebox .... 72 sq. ft

Total ....929 sq. ft
Grate Area ....13 sq. ft
Boiler Pressure ....120 lbs per sq. in.
Weight in working order ....32 tons 10 cwt

The North London Railway sold the engine in 1873 to the Whitehaven Colliery Co. from whom it was acquired, as already mentioned, by the Colne Valley & Halstead Railway on which it was known as No. 2. This number, however, was never actually painted on to the engine and was reserved for use in the Company's records. The Colne Valley removed the original copper topped chimney and substituted a stove pipe pattern and a cab was built to give increased protection to the crew who had hitherto relied on a front weatherboard for their only shelter. The locomotive was sold in 1894 to the South Hetton Colliery but survived only until 1902, when it was withdrawn.

When it became necessary to provide replacements for the *Brewster* and *Halstead* in 1887 two 2–4–2 inside cylinder side-tank engines were built for the line by Hawthorn, Leslie and Co. Ltd (Works No. 2079 and 2080). The design was neat but undistinguished and had something of Great Eastern practice in it. They were a great advance on any engines the Company has hitherto possessed and for the first time for years locomotives were available that were masters of the loads they were called upon to handle. The new locomotives were capable of hauling twenty-four loaded wagons over the gradients between Yeldham and Haverhill, whereas the 0–4–2 tank engine No. 1 could handle only fourteen. The satisfaction given by these engines led to the purchase of a third in 1894 from the same makers (Works No. 2283). At first no numbers were carried except the works numbers which were painted on the buffer beams and they were known by the names *Halstead, Colne* and *Hedingham* respectively which were carried on brass plates on the tank-sides. After some fifteen years or so they were, however, given the Nos. 2, 3 and 4.[2]

The original boilers were in three rings with the dome on the middle ring but all three were subsequently rebuilt at the Stratford Works of the Great Eastern Railway with slightly larger boilers in two rings with the dome on the front ring; No. 2, *Halstead* in 1896; No. 3 *Colne* in 1897 and No. 4 *Hedingham* in 1902. The following table gives the principal dimensions;

Cylinders ....16 in. x 24 in.
Coupled wheels ....5 ft 1 in. diameter
Leading and trailing wheels .....3 ft 2 in. diameter

	Before rebuilding	After rebuilding
Heating Surface:		
Tubes	849 sq. ft	961.13 sq. ft
Firebox	70 sq. ft	77.36 sq. ft
Total	919 sq. ft	1038.49 sq. ft
Boiler Pressure	–	140 lbs per sq. in.
Weight in		
working order	43 tons	44 tons 12 cwts

It would seem that they all had stovepipe chimneys when received, later to be changed for copper-tops. No. 2 (*Halstead*) during one of its visits to Stratford Works managed to acquire a Great Eastern suburban tank engine smoke-box door, complete with brackets for carrying destination name-boards. It also received a Great Eastern type safety-valve casing, as did the others in the trio.

The Colne Valley locomotive stock, even with the addition of these engines, was barely sufficient for its requirements and left no real reserve for emergencies. In addition the gradual increase of goods traffic, particularly the haulage of bricks from the brickyards at Purls Hill and Hedingham necessitated a larger and more powerful locomotive. The appointment of Mr Hawkins as General Manager in 1903 brought with it a number of reforms in the locomotive department, of which the most important was probably the decision to abolish as far as possible the practice of hiring locomotives from the Great Eastern Railway when Colne Valley locomotives were under repair. This was effected in part by the reorganization of the repair facilities and their transfer from Haverhill to Halstead, which is referred to again later on, but this measure was not a complete palliative and succeeded only in reducing the frequency of the hirings. It was clear, therefore, that from every point of view fresh locomotive power was becoming more and more necessary and the Directors at length sanctioned the purchase of a new engine from Messrs Hudswell, Clarke & Co. of Leeds. This was delivered in 1908 (Works No. 836) and became No. 5.

It was an inside cylindered 0–6–2 side-tank engine of modest proportions, not greatly in excess of those of the earlier 2–4–2s but better adapted for goods working. The dimensions were:

Cylinders ....16 in. x 24 in.
Coupled Wheels ....4 ft 6 in. diameter
Trailing Wheels ....3 ft 8 in. diameter

Heating Surface:

Tubes ....887.2 sq. ft

Firebox .... 87.2 sq. ft

Total ....974.4 sq. ft

Grate Area ....14.65 sq. ft

Boiler Pressure ....150 lbs per sq. in.

Weight in working order ....50 tons 3 cwts

The engine was hailed by the *Halstead Gazette* as follows:

They have just added to their rolling stock a fine new engine, built by Messrs Hudswell, Clarke & Co. Ltd, (one of the best firms of locomotive builders in the world) whose works are at Leeds. It is a "six-wheel couple" (sic!), a system that is largely used in Wales for hill climbing. It is fitted up with all the latest improvements. This addition to the Company's engines will enable all repairs to the others to be carried out without any inconvenience.

No further locomotives were acquired by the Colne Valley and Halstead Railway and the working of the line was carried out by Nos. 2, 3, 4 and 5, with No. 1 as spare engine, until the date of the absorption into the LNER. In the latter days of the Company a livery of black, relieved by a vermilion line, was adopted. The 2–4–2s at one time carried the letters CV in gilt on the tank sides but the 0–6–2, when new, bore "CV and HR" in much smaller letters lower down the tank sides and retained this lettering for several years.

The early coaches of the Colne Valley were supplied by Messrs J. Wright & Sons, of Saltley, Birmingham, who were predecessors of the Metropolitan Railway Carriage & Wagon Co. Originally the total strength consisted of eight vehicles only, namely four thirds, two firsts and second composites and two brakes which were delivered in 1859. Two more composites and a futher brake of the same design were bought in 1863. The coaches were straight sided and had very low roofs. Internally they were not fitted with transverse seats in the usual manner but had seats, (wooden ones in the thirds), arranged round the walls. The length over headstocks was 18 ft 6 in. or slightly more than the length of the open wagon of present day Railway Clearing House design. The last of these coaches ran until about 1903 and a body which the authors believe may have belonged to one of these vehicles at present serves as a waiting room at White Colne Station.

Their successors were seven six–wheelers comprised of two thirds built by the Lancaster Railway Carriage & Wagon Company Ltd. and bought in 1897; two thirds built by the Metropolitan Railway Carriage & Wagon Company Ltd. and bought in 1899; a brake third and a composite built in the Midland Railway's shops bought second-hand through a firm of dealers, of which the date of purchase is uncertain; and a composite purchased in 1887, of which the builder cannot be traced. These coaches each contained five compartments, lit by colza oil lamps and seating ten passengers in the third class and six in the first class. Later Mr Hawkins equipped them with acetylene gas lighting. The bodies were 31 ft 6 in. long except in the case of the pair manufactured by the Lancaster Railway Carriage & Wagon Company which were 6 in. longer.

The final acquisition by the Company came from a rather curious source. In 1906 Mr Hawkins, the General Manager paid a visit to Lillie Bridge depôt on the Metropolitan District Railway in order to inspect a number of old four-wheeled coaches which had been withdrawn from service and were being offered for sale. He had found nothing suitable and was preparing to leave when he noticed some coaches, protected by dust-sheets, in one corner of the sheds. More from curiosity than anything he enquired what they were. When they were shown to him they proved to be the three coaches of the multiple unit electric train which ran experimentally between Earl's Court and South Kensington in 1900. In response to his query he was told that if no more experiments were to be conducted the Company might consider disposing of them and his guide suggested that he should submit a written enquiry. Shortly after his return to Halstead he wrote a letter to the Metropolitan District Railway asking if the coaches were for sale. He received a reply asking him to make an offer. Without consulting the Board, Mr Hawkins sent an answer pointing out that owing to its special construction the third coach was practically scrap and offered £250. He was told in reply that if he would increase his offer to £275 the coaches were his. Unfortunately for Mr Hawkin's peace of mind the Board were not meeting for another three weeks, during which time he was on tenterhooks for fear that a better offer might be made. However, no such calamity came to pass and he was authorised to make the purchase. Accordingly the Colne Valley & Halstead Railway became the possessors of a multiple unit electric train in more or less working order.

The alterations to two of the coaches were of a minor character and the trials of the converted vehicles, one of six compartments and the other seven, took place on Monday 22nd October, 1906. The third coach of the set, a composite brake was not placed in commission until April 1908, as the modifications required were more extensive. A peculiarity of the tractive equipment of the train was that the armatures were wound directly onto the bogie axles. The two ends of the main frame of the third coach had been set up to take these large bogies and it was necessary to remove the bogies and build down the

A fine view of the old single-driver Well Tank locomotive acquired from the LBSC Railway seen here outside the original shed at Halstead.

Authors' Collection

Brewster, 2–4–0 tank engine built by Manning Wardle in 1861. Two others, *Halstead* and *Colne* were similar, none received numbers.

LRGP, Courtesy David & Charles

0–6–0T locomotive, formerly No. 10 of the Cornwall Minerals Railway, later named *Haverhill*, was built by Sharp Stewart in 1873 and sold 1889 to S. Hutton Colliery Co. where it worked until 1948. *Authors' Collection*

No. 4 *Hedingham* 2–4–2T.   *Author's Collection*

No. 5, the last locomotive purchased by the CV & H Railway in 1908. A very handsome workman-like 0–6–2T built by Hudswell Clark & Co. seen here as delivered but the locomotive was not given a name.   *Authors' Collection*

A later view of No. 5 showing the Westinghouse pump but now devoid of its lining out and owner's initials, probably in plain war-time black.

LGRP, Courtesy David & Charles

Locomotive No. 5 ex-CV&H Railway, 0–6–2T after the take-over by the LNER. Now No. 8314, class 'N18' and still looking quite smart.

LGRP, Courtesy David & Charles

10 TON WAGON NO. 24

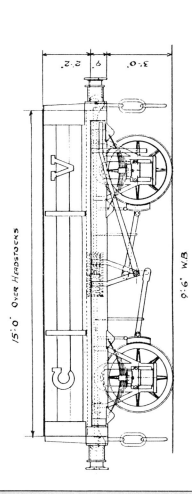

8 TON WAGON NO. 46

COLOUR—DULL GREY

By kind permission of K.A. Werrett

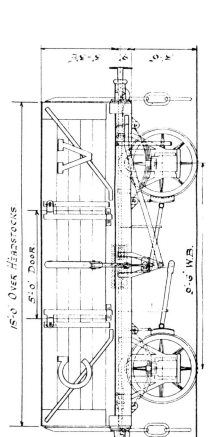

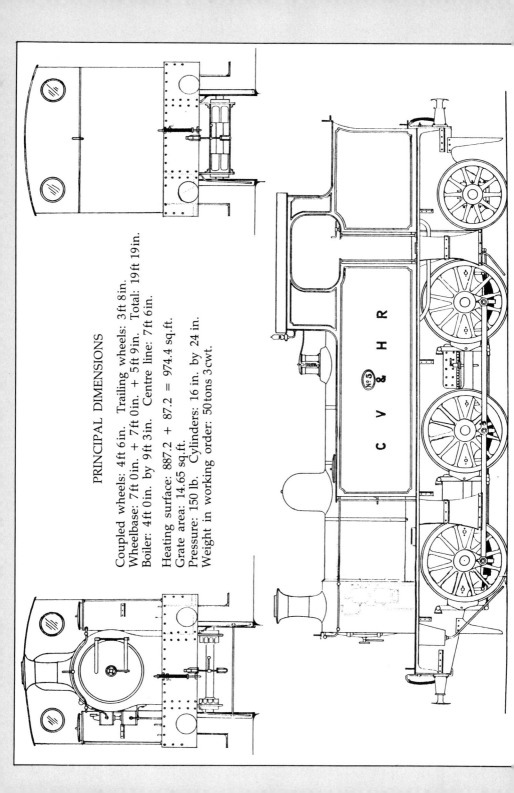

PRINCIPAL DIMENSIONS

Coupled wheels: 4 ft 6 in.   Trailing wheels: 3 ft 8 in.
Wheelbase: 7 ft 0 in. + 7 ft 0 in. + 5 ft 9 in.   Total: 19 ft 19 in.
Boiler: 4 ft 0 in. by 9 ft 3 in.   Centre line: 7 ft 6 in.

Heating surface: 887.2 + 87.2 = 974.4 sq.ft.
Grate area: 14.65 sq.ft.
Pressure: 150 lb.   Cylinders: 16 in. by 24 in.
Weight in working order: 50 tons 3 cwt.

frames with rolled steel joists to take the new pressed steel framed bogies which were ordered from the Metropolitan Railway Carriage & Wagon Company, the builders of the coaches in the first place. The high prices obtained for the scrap helped to offset the cost of the alterations and the conversions generally had been so economical that Mr Hawkins was able to persuade the Board to allow him to equip all three coaches with electric lighting on Stone's system before they were placed into service. The three converted vehicles formed an extremely handsome train for their time and the Company's action was loudly applauded in the local press. The *Halstead Gazette* remarked that "We think the public should warmly appreciate the enterprise and progressive policy of the Colne Valley Company; they are doing their best to meet the requirements of the public and it must not be forgotten they are hemmed in at both ends of their system." The bodies of these coaches were 39 ft 6 in. long. As in the six-wheelers ten third class passengers were carried in each compartment but the seating capacity of the first class compartments was increased from six to eight.

The passenger train stock was completed by a six-wheeled brake van built by the Metropolitan Railway Carriage and Wagon Co. and purchased in 1899, two other brake vans and a horse-box.

The return attached to the Company's report dated 30th June, 1868 gives the freight rolling stock as 24 open wagons, 2 covered wagons, 2 timber vans and 1 travelling crane. By the end of the century the line possessed 109 wagons of various types. A description of the line published in November 1901, gives the number as 149, the increase being accounted for by the fact that at that time wagons were being acquired to deal with the brick traffic from Hedingham which required from 30 to 40 wagons daily. This figure of 149 was made up of 118 open wagons, nine covered wagons, nine timber wagons, ten cattle wagons, one travelling crane and two ballast wagons. At the time of the amalgamation the goods stock consisted of 174 wagons and 1 service vehicle (the crane), the total comprising 143 open wagons, 9 covered wagons, 3 "special" wagons, 10 cattle trucks, 6 timber trucks, and 3 brake vans. The wagons were built variously by Messrs. Harris & Cam, the Lancaster Wagon Company, the Metropolitan Wagon Company, the Birmingham Wagon Company and Craven Brothers.

The livery of the passenger rolling stock was originaly a shade known officially as "drab" picked out with thin black and yellow lines. First class compartments were upholstered in blue and thirds in brown although it has already been noticed that not all the thirds had upholstery. The coaches were lettered "CVR" in small letters on the panels. With the introduction of the ex-Metropolitan District coaches this livery was varied to varnished teak, the words "Colne Valley Railway" being painted in large letters above the windows and the Company's coat of arms transferred on to the lower panels. The goods stock was painted grey and lettered in white.

Other minor items of railway rolling stock were two "rail-cycles". These products of American ingenuity each consisted broadly of two pairs of pressed steel wheels and axles of the type used for platelayers' trollies coupled together by a light tubular frame fitted with a pair of handlebars and a saddle for the rider. The motive power was supplied by a pair of pedals driving the rear axle in a manner similar to that employed in old fashioned tricycles. A number of these rail cycles are still used by the Great Southern Railway of Ireland but the Colne Valley specimens have long since disappeared. During their life they were principally used for inspection purposes, and by the staff for travelling between stations when no locomotive was available.

Apart from its railway vehicles the Colne Valley possessed six (latterly eight) drays and horses for their local deliveries in Halstead, and one horse for shunting. It used to be a regular practice of the Colne Valley to mow the grass on the embankments and cuttings and to make hay of it for the feeding of these horses. The hay was collected by a special train, taken to Earls Colne station where plenty of space was available and stacked. This was not the only side of the Colne Valley's agricultureal activity. On the waterlogged ground adjacent to Earl's Colne Yard beds of osiers were grown and cut regularly while other waste ground was used to grow willows. Possibly, however, "agricultural" is not quite accurate as a description of this enterprise and it might be more suitably called "arboricultural".

---

[1] Quoting from the builders' records.

[2] The numbers were cast in brass and applied to the bunker sides and the name-plates were removed from the side-tanks. After Mr Hawkins took charge the numbers were removed and the name-plates restored.

Example of Colne Valley Railway luggage label.

Chapter Six

The Operating Department

The train service provided by the Colne Valley & Halstead Railway can be summarized as four trains in each direction each weekday, and two in each direction on Sundays.[1] It is not proposed, therefore, to give extended details of such slight variations as occurred but representative timetables are given in *Appendix C*. Indeed, almost the only noteworthy variation took place in November 1921, when, as a result of a steady loss on Sunday trains, it was decided to discontinue them altogether.

The Colne Valley was always generous in its provision of excursion trains and during the summer of 1861 it advertised excursions to Ipswich and Harwich to run every Sunday. The trains departed from Castle Hedingham (the present Sible and Castle Hedingham) and called at all Colne Valley stations from which standard fares of 5/-, 3/6 and 2/6 respectively for first, second and third class were charged. On the return journey the trains left Harwich at 4.25 pm and Ipswich at 4.45 pm.

At the same time, it advertised Sunday return fares at the price of a single journey between its own stations, and to Sudbury, Bures, Colchester and intermediate stations to Ipswich and Harwich, while on Saturdays similar fares applied between Colne Valley stations but not to any (including Chappel) on the Eastern Counties Railway. The facilities thus provided gave many people the opportunity of travelling beyond the confines of their own and the adjoining parishes for the first time, and the response was extremely gratifying to the railway company. It was not equally welcomed by the local clergy, who found that they frequently suffered an alarming diminution in their congregations. A petition was organised to bring the excursions to an end and an attempt was even made to end Sunday trains altogether. It was unsuccessful but, as on the occasion of other disputes, verbal missiles were exchanged with considerable violence and letters for and against the petition inundated the local papers.

Other early cheap fare facilities were available to London. By arrangement with the Eastern Counties Railway a train left London at 12.30 pm on Wednesdays during 1861 on which the return fares to the Colne Valley stations were respectively 10/-, 7/6 and 5/3 for three classes. The corresponding up-train left Castle Hedingham on Fridays at 8.10 am and the return half of a ticket was available either on the Friday following the outward journey or the next Friday after that. Similar arrangements, of course, operated in the reverse direction using the same trains.

The Colne Valley ran a number of excursions in connection with the Exhibition held in Kensington in 1862. Although this was called the "Great" Exhibition, it was but a poor shadow of its predecessor of 1851 and was open only from 1st May–1st November. On a humbler plane a train was also run, in conjunction with the Great Eastern Railway, to the Agricultural Show at Brentwood on 2nd March, 1865. With the completion of the connecting line between the two railways at Haverhill, the Colne Valley ran the first of a series of excursions to Cambridge on 28th September, 1865. The "long expected and eagerly awaited excursion", as a local paper called it, received an unusual degree of attention even for that time. Halstead observed the day more or less as a public holiday and most of the shops closed for the occasion, while some people near the station decorated their houses with flags and streamers. As the 28th was a Thursday, the staff of the *Halstead Gazette* might not have been able to participate in the trip had not the Editor kindly brought it out a day earlier than usual so that they too could take part. The excursionists returned late that day duly impressed, we are told, by the visit to the great seat of learning.

In later years it was the practice to run three or four half day excursions every year to Clacton. These were very popular and successful. The Colne Valley management generally contrived to arrange them near the time of full moons so as to give the country folk plenty of light to get home by.

Road competition in those days was, of course, no serious matter but a Mr Smith, owner of a livery stable in Halstead, ran a horse 'bus to Braintree on Wednesdays and to Colchester on Tuesdays and Saturdays. Braintree could be approached by rail only by an extremely circuitous journey but the trip to Colchester was much easier and with the introduction of cheap tickets on the railway, the number of passengers on the horse 'bus showed an alarming decline and first the Tuesday and then the Saturday journey was suspended. Mr John Cook, the local common carrier, also carried passengers to Colchester on Wednesdays and Saturdays in winter and on Mondays, Wednesdays and Saturdays in summer. As the cart took three and a half hours on the journey, its patronage was limited.

The first Appendix to the Working Timetable was not compiled until 1905, but it clearly set out, often for the first time, many details concerning the working of trains. The Colne Valley head-codes, for instance, were very simple. All ordinary passenger and goods trains carried one red light at the foot of the chimney and one white light on the left hand buffer beam (i.e. the left hand as viewed from the footplate) while special trains carried a red light at the foot of the chimney and a white light over each buffer, the corresponding lamps being carried unlighted by day. Other matters clarified by the new

Appendix were the system of engine whistles and the use and codes on the telegraph circuits. Insignificant as the issue of this document appears, it represented in reality a great step forward. It has already been noticed when discussing the signalling that grave irregularities in working were practically an every day occurrence until the appointment of Mr Hawkins and the compilation of the Appendix was one step in the far-reaching reorganization which he found necessary.

Not the least obstacle in the way of enforcing strictly the rules for single line working was the distressing number of failures of the electric telegraph apparatus. It was apparently the custom for the Manager to assume personally the responibility of sending the trains forward without proper protection, but Mr Hawkins made pilot working the rule on such occasions. In so doing, however, he aroused a certain amount of antagonism in the regular travellers who complained that "slight" failures of this kind had never caused such delays under the old regime!

Until 1903 no proper register of locomotives and rolling stock was kept. It was a comparatively easy task to compile one showing the locomotives and passenger coaches, but the wagons presented far more difficulties. Fortunately the wagon examiner was an intelligent type of man and had a rough list for his own use: by checking the particulars shown on this list as the wagons returned to the parent system and amplifying it as necessary a record was built up. Matters were complicated by the fact that many wagons had been broken up without the fact being recorded so that the reconciliation of the actual figures with those on the returns presented some difficulties.

After this came the task of standardisation. Formerly, wagons had often to stand for weeks when a part was being repaired while in the event of a breakdown on a foreign line, it was frequently necessary to stop a similar wagon at Halstead (if indeed, there was one of similar type), and rob it of the part required. The fitting of new standard springs, axleboxes and in some cases, buffers, to such old wagons as merited the expense, enabled a small stock of spares to be assembled, and, at the same time, the use of some wagons which were in a bad way was limited to journeys between Colne Valley stations.

The changes did not pass without comment from the staff, but they soon found that when the most urgent innovations in operating methods had been made, the new Manager was equally willing to institute reforms for their benefit. All the traffic staff, enginemen, guards and platform staff were rated as seven day men when he took over, taking turns for Sunday work without overtime. At the same time, increases in wages had been given haphazardly, with the result that anomalies and petty jealousies had arisen. However, about 1907 Mr Hawkins persuaded the Board to introduce a six day week and simultaneously to adopt the standard rates of pay used by the Great Eastern Railway on its adjoining lines of similar character. These measures brought about an increase in earnings for almost all the men employed.

At this period, the Colne Valley men were non-unionists, but during the 1914–18 war they nearly all joined one or other of the railway unions. The introduction of new rates of pay in 1920–21 by agreement between the railway companies and the trade unions imposed such a burden on the finances of the line that it became necessary either to reduce the staff, or to lower their wages. In response to a personal appeal by the Manager the men, as already noticed in the historical chapter, accepted a 10% cut in their rates of pay. Meanwhile a rigorous economy campaign had been put into operation, part of which was the cancellation of the unremunerative Sunday trains and the results so far exceeded expectations that the pay cut was restored by the end of 1921.

The Colne Valley was party to the Railway Clearing House from 1859 and was also a member of the Railway Companies' Association. In this connection it should be mentioned that in more recent times the Officers and Board of the Great Eastern Railway extended their help toward their small neighbour in a very liberal degree, even to the extent of lending Mr Hawkins an inspection saloon for the annual visit of the Directors to the line.

To close this brief account of operating matters on a lighter note, it may be interesting to quote Mr Hawkins' reasons for changing the name of Colne Station to Earls Colne. As he remarked:"I thought it time for this to be done after we had received, amongst other things, a cab intended for Colne Lancashire together with boxes of bullion for the same town and a truck load of pigs for Calne in Wiltshire."

---

[1] Except for a short period about 1908, when the service was increased to Five in each direction on weekdays, with SEVEN on Saturdays. Also, there were THREE trains for a short time on Sundays a few years earlier.

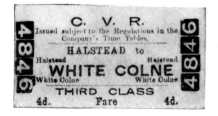

Examples of Colne Valley & Halstead Railway tickets. Note the abbreviated initials of title. First class were white, and Thirds were buff. *From collection of late Fred. H. Smith.*

Chapter Seven
Accidents and Incidents

The Colne Valley & Halstead Railway enjoyed a commendable immunity from accidents throughout its career but did not escape them entirely, though only one passenger lost his life as a result, the victim being a child who was playing with an inside door handle, with the result that the door opened and he fell on to the track.

The earliest train accident of which a record survives[1] occurred at Yeldham on 20th January, 1877, when a pair of horses belonging to a Mr Francis Whitlock were being driven across the track. The leading horse was struck and killed by an oncoming train but the carters had the presence of mind to jump clear and so escape injury. After this accident it was made a rule that a warning whistle should be given by trains approaching the crossing, which was on a curve.

The sheltered Essex countryside through which the Colne Valley & Halstead Railway ran experiences serious snowdrifts only on comparatively rare occasions but on the evening of 18th January, 1881, after a snow storm, a train became set fast in a drift near Chappel, having to remain there the whole night, while the passengers made their way to shelter as best they could. Next day it was rescued by a gang of navvies armed with shovels.

The weather played another rather peculiar trick on the Colne Valley in August 1902, this time as a result of a thunderstorm. A locomotive driver named Salmon had placed his hand on the regulator handle of his locomotive when he was struck by lightning. He was fortunate enough to escape serious injury but the experience caused his absence from work for several days.

An incident of a more intriguing character took place at Hedingham on 9th May, 1887. The permanent way ganger of that section, a man named Allen, was returning along the track after his dinner, shortly before one o'clock, when he discovered a man lying with his head upon one of the rails. His first reaction, not unnaturally, was astonishment, but it took him very little time to realise that he had a would-be suicide to deal with, though one who had chosen his time badly as no train was due until two o'clock. Allen having found him, it was quite another matter to alter his purpose and his resolve was still unabated when two o'clock arrived. Allen, therefore, proceeded in the direction from which the train was coming and succeeded in halting it. He returned with the driver, Sam Plum, to the "suicide" who was still assiduously keeping his head on the rail, and, enlisting the aid of a third man, a Mr Slaughter, they forcibly removed him from the path of the train, committing him to the care of the local constabulary.

The only serious accident that happened on the Colne Valley occurred on the evening of the 8th December, 1899. The driver of the evening up goods train, which had been standing on the down passing loop at Halstead station, started his train while the signals were against him and the points set for the sidings. It will be seen on referring to the plan of Halstead station (*page 43*) that a long siding runs parallel to the running line as far as the Parsonage Street level crossing, and along this the goods train proceeded at increaing speed. Everyone present realised that a smash was inevitable, except the driver, who remained blissfully unaware of his error. As the train approached the buffer stops, Henry Kibble, the gatekeeper, waved his hand lamp frantically in a vain effort to attract the attention of the crew, who, however, continued on their way quite oblivious of what was impending. The engine took the buffer stops in its stride, smashed its way through the gates and finally embedded itself in the signal box on the other side of the road. Four wagons of the dozen or more making up the train were completely wrecked, one being loaded with flour, which was scattered very liberally over a large number of live chickens that had escaped from an adjacent wagon. The effect as they fled squawking into the darkness must have been not a little bizarre. Many of them, it is said, found their way into the hands, and ultimately the kitchens, of the local populace, who had been drawn to the scene of the incident.[2]

The driver and fireman involved in this discreditable affair, Messrs H. Bartholomew and J. Roope, were lucky enough to escape practically uninjured. The locomotive was not seriously damaged, the buffers and the bunker being the only parts to suffer to any extent. The running line was, of course, blocked and a Great Eastern Railway breakdown gang had to be called to clear up the wreckage. Whilst the work was in progress trains worked up to either side and the passengers crossed the gap on foot.

One particularly dirty night towards the end of 1903, Mr Hawkins, the Manager, had just settled himself by the fireside when a messenger arrived from the station to say that the up goods from Haverhill was derailed about a quarter of a mile short of Halstead station. Rejecting the suggestion that the Great Eastern breakdown gang be called, Mr Hawkins mustered some of his own men and set off for the spot, the party taking with them the jacks and packing they required. The "disaster" proved to be one old Colne Valley truck, loaded with bricks, which had all wheels off the road, and the following truck, which had one pair off. The gang quickly had these re-railed but as soon as they moved the train the old Colne Valley truck jumped off again. On examination it was found that the axle guard was out of line. Mr Hawkins, therefore, had the bricks unloaded and turned the wagon over down a low embankment, picking it up next day.

If there is little to record of accidents, the field of incidents is more fruitful. No small line exists for long without accumulating a fund of humorous anecdotes concerning itself and the Colne Valley was by no means an exception. Probably the most intriguing happening of all is recorded in the *Halstead Gazette* report on an excursion to Cambridge on 27th September, 1878. The passengers had completed their exploration of the borough and were drifting back to their seats on the Colne Valley train when one of their number who had made the outward journey alone, returned to the train with a small girl. He astonished his fellow passengers by informing them that he had purchased the child and was taking her home with him. Just before the departure time, a man appeared on the platform and began to argue with the supposed purchaser. The conversation is not recorded but it is known that a half-crown changed hands and the excursionist left for home with his new acquisition.

The Colne Valley Railway had no extravagant ideas regarding salaries in its early days. In March, 1868, Thomas Mackay, who had been employed as Station-master at Colne left after a disagreement with the management whom he subsequently sued for the sum of £4 2s. 10d., the amount of his salary from 1st to 22nd March at the rate of five pounds a month, i.e., £3 12s. 0d. plus a fine of 10/-, which had been deducted for alleged misconduct leading to his dismissal and tenpence expended on postage. Five pounds a month for a Station-master is scarcely overpayment, but it needs to be pointed out that Colne (the present White Colne station) needed only one person to carry out the combined duties of a complete station staff, so that the work cannot have been as onerous as might be imagined.

Close by Chappel station there was, until the necessities of war demanded that it be ploughed up, a large meadow on which, years ago, the lads of the village, among whom could be numbered the young porters from the station, used to play football on Saturday afternoons. One point about these games, however, which made them unique among village football was the "Sudbury train rule", which was devised to reconcile the conflicting claims of athletics and the working of the railway. It was an unfortunate fact that a train was due to arrive from Sudbury at 3.34 and a Colne Valley train in connection two minutes earlier. To overcome the difficulty of dealing with the two trains without interfering with the game, it was laid down that as soon as the home signal was lowered, the referee was to blow his whistle for half-time, when the station staff would hurriedly climb over the fence, run into the porters' room, don their uniform trousers and jackets and deal with the trains. As soon as the latter had been joined together and had left for Marks Tey, the second half of the match would be played.

Kings Road, Halstead, forms the north-west boundary of the former Colne Valley property, from which it is separated by a wooden fence. Opposite one house, however, it gives place to a brick wall as high as the front of the house itself. The reason for this is rather interesting and not incurious. The house whose outlook is thus curtailed was formerly the private residence of Mr A.W. Kibble, one-time manager of the Tortoise Foundry, Halstead. In 1900 a dispute arose between the latter company and the Colne Valley concerning the use of the foundry siding for the loading of heavy castings and other ironwork, which culminated in the railway forcing the foundry company to haul the goods into the station yard and ship them there, thereby entailing a wasteful and expensive short haul by horse-drawn vehicles. Broadly speaking the dispute arose from a clause in the Company's Act which stipulated that no shunting should take place over the Trinity Street level crossing and no train should be allowed to stand on the crossing while trucks were being shunted, which was interpreted by Mr Copus, the then Manager, as barring the use of the Tortoise Foundary siding altogether. The matter was finally settled before the Railway Commissioners in 1901 by a compromise, each of the contestants being ordered to bear their own costs. Unfortunately, Mr George Copus took the partial defeat as a personal affront and commenced what was tantamount to a persecution of Mr Kibble. He gave vent to some of his malice by having a high wall, against which he built a lean-to shed, erected immediately in front of Mr Kibble's house, so that all the front windows overlooked a blank wall. To add insult to injury Mr Copus permitted the wall to be used for all types of posters, and so, the story goes, actually encouraged billposting thereon by letting the space for 10/- per annum. The townspeople readily recognized the purpose of the new shed and dubbed it the "spite wall" by which name it is still known. When Mr Hawkins succeeded Mr Copus, he endeavoured to lessen the inconvenience by ordering the removal of all the bills and prohibiting fresh ones, but the wall and shed still stand and at present are used by a firm of coal merchants. The siding remained closed for two years or so after the arrival of Mr Hawkins but he eventually persuaded the Directors to reopen it and it has remained in use without complaint from anyone concerned.

---

[1] Except for a minor accident at Colne (now White Colne) crossing on 1st January, 1864, when an up morning train not stopping at Colne demolished the crossing gates, which had been left shut against the train by an error on the part of the gate-keeper.

[2] *see page 84.*

Chapter Eight

Under New Management

As one might expect from its location, the Colne Valley became a part of the Great Eastern section of the LNER from 1st January, 1923. At first the outward signs of the change were scarcely apparent, but observant users of the line may have remarked on the withdrawal of two passenger brake vans and a horse box in June 1923. They were followed to the scrap-heap in July by coaches 14 and 16 and two of the ex-Midland six-wheelers and thereafter the whole of the passenger rolling stock was gradually withdrawn. The only coaches scheduled for further use by the LNER were Nos. 11 and 12, the surviving parts of the three coach train set purchased from the Metropolitan District Railway, the third coach of the set, No. 13, a brake third, having been almost totally destroyed by fire in the latter days of the Colne Valley. For these two vehicles the respite was very brief and they too were withdrawn shortly afterwards.

On the locomotive side changes were also afoot. It has already been noticed that the locomotives in use at the time the LNER took over were the 0–4–2T, No. 1; the three 2–4–2Ts, No. 2, 3 and 4, and the 0–6–2T, No. 5. It is believed that the class designation 'Z6' was intended for No. 1 but it was never applied as the veteran was withdrawn almost immediately. Later on in the same year No. 4 was scrapped. The two remaining 2–4–2Ts, however, received the LNER classification 'F9', and lasted for several years longer. No. 3 (renumbered 8313) continued in use until 1927 and No. 2 (renumbered 8312) the oldest of the trio, until as late as 1930. The 0–6–2T, No. 5, was renumbered 8314 and became Class 'N18' and ended its days shunting at Colchester, where it worked until 1928.

The end of independence meant also the end of the Head Office at Halstead station and the cessation of the other activities that had marked the headquarters of the line. The modest locomotive and carriage workshops were first closed and then denuded of their equipment. A few of the machines were sent to Ipswich but the majority became scrap. Finally the buildings were demolished. With the watchful eyes of Mr Hawkins gone, there was no longer any point in maintaining a locomotive running shed at Halstead and this too was closed and demolished, its remaining functions being transferred to the shed at Haverhill.

In the interests, both of economy and expediency, it was decided to close the passenger station of the Colne Valley at Haverhill (or Haverhill South as it was designated by the LNER) and to terminate all Colne Valley passenger trains at Haverhill North (the Great Eastern station). Subsequently the buildings of the passenger station

Colne Valley and Halstead Railway Company.

I am desired to give you Notice that a Special General Meeting of the proprietors and Debenture Stock Holders of this Company will, in accordance with the Railways Act, 1921, be held at No. 144, Palmerston House, Bishopsgate, London, E.C., 2, on Monday, the 26th day of March, 1923, at twelve o'clock noon, for the purpose of considering and, if thought fit, of approving a Scheme in pursuance of the said Act for the absorption of this Company and other Railway Companies by the London and North Eastern Railway Company.

I am also desired to give you Notice that immediately after the conclusion of the said Special General Meeting, an extraordinary Meeting of the Proprietors of the Company will be held at the same place, for the purpose of determining, (if the Scheme above referred to be approved) pursuant to the said Scheme, the amount of compensation to be paid, out of the assets of the Company, to the Directors of the Company, who suffer loss by abolition of Office.

The Scheme provides that Stock of the London and North Eastern Railway Company is to be issued in exchange for the Debenture Stocks of this Company and that payment in cash shall be made to the holders of shares of this Company on the following basis :—

Colne Valley and Halstead Railway Company's Capital.	London & North Eastern Railway Company's Stocks to be issued (or cash to be paid) in exchange.
For each £100 5% "A" Debenture Stock £100 4% "B" Debenture Stock £ 10 Preference Share £ 10 Ordinary Share.	£125 4% First Preference Stock £ 10 5% Preferred Ordinary Stock 3s. cash 2s 6d. cash.

I enclose herewith blank form of Proxy for use at the Special General Meeting.

ELYOT S. HAWKINS,
Secretary.

Secretary's Office,
   Halstead, Essex,
      7th, March 1923.

This was probably the last official notice to be issued by the Colne Valley and Halstead Railway before the final liquidation.

were demolished and the platforms removed. Haverhill South, however, continues to be used as a goods depot.

Although the Colne Valley had begun to convert its permanent way from flat-bottomed rail to bull headed the process was far from complete in 1923 and was carried on by the LNER. The last length of flat-bottomed track to remain in use on the running lines was at a point near Earls Colne but this was finally replaced, in 1934, since when the only flat-bottomed rail has been in sidings. The replacements have been variously with 80 lbs, 85 lbs and 95 lbs per yard rail, most of it second-hand from the main lines of the LNER.

The Colne Valley stationery was very soon replaced by that of the LNER but a few of the larger items such as ledgers survived for a few years. At Yeldham the pre-group Abstract Book remained in use for some time but the authors were amused to note that the clerk has been careful to cross through the heading "Colne Valley Railway" on each page and substitute, in pencil, "LNER". Other small items such as sign-boards and warning notices, were, in the course of time, replaced by the new standard types so that it is now very difficult to find evidence of the existence of a small but interesting component part of the LNER.

Such aspirations as the good folk of East Anglia may have entertained of receiving an improved railway service under the new regime brought about as a result of the "grouping" at 1923 which placed their lines with the new London & North Eastern Railway proved to be entirely misplaced. Excepting the acceleration of a few prestige main line services and a few expresses to important holiday resorts, rural branches and cross-country lines appear to have been entirely overlooked by the LNER. It has to be said that the trains neither got faster nor more frequent, though the rolling stock employed may have marginally improved over the years, but punctuality tended to slip. The following tabulation shows the average journey time in minutes required to cover the 56 miles between Halstead and Liverpool Street and vice versa by the four or five trains which departed at about the same hours throughout:

	1883	1908	1914	1921	1927	1932	1938	1955	1960	
Up trains:	113	121	112	129	128	125	128	124	138	mins
Down trains:	124	131	118	129	132	134	129	139	117	

The above figures make pretty dismal reading considering that 47 of the 56 mile journey was over a main line. 1914 was the only year showing any better timings than those obtaining in 1883 at which date both the CV&H and the GE railways were in very low water financially. It should be noted that the apparent great improvement in the Down train times for 1960 (after dieselisation) is entirely due to the insertion of a positioning non-stop run up the branch (see time-table), – otherwise the figure would have read 136. It can be observed that in 1938 after 15 years under the LNER nothing had changed, no attempt was made to restore the 1914 pre-war timings, and that by 1955 under BR the service had definitely worsened, yet from 1951 there was a train from Liverpool Street to Norwich every hour which covered the 115 miles in from 123 to 130 minutes!

The Colne Valley Company could only offer a train service that connected with whatever the GER and its successors chose to provide at either end. It could be said however, that in CV/GE days the service was extremely reliable and punctual. Unfortunately there were always certain basic defects in the service offered which persisted throughout, notably (a) a business man desiring to reach Halstead by 10.00 am would need to present himself at Liverpool Street at the ungodly hour of 6.45 am: the next departure at 10.00 am would not get him to Halstead until 11.45; and (b) having completed his business, if he did not catch the 2.35 pm Up train he had perforce to fill in time as best he might until after 6.30 pm; (c) the first Down departure from Halstead did not proceed farther than the Hedinghams so nobody could reach Haverhill earlier than 12.30 pm. This was remedied by the LNER about 1938 by extending the early departure through to Haverhill, but nothing whatsoever was done to improve the other defects.

After the 1914–1918 war the great upsurge in the use of the automobile for private use or as public transport steadily drew passengers away from the railway. Would be investors in motor-bus operation were quick to notice any weak points in the railway facilities, and provide services and make profits with the Colne Valley line being particularly vulnerable: Colchester was the natural place to which residents gravitated for all important business, shopping and its markets, but going by train required one and often two changes, and having reached Colchester station they were still a long way from town centre which required a tram journey and the extra fare or a very long uphill walk if a taxicab was too expensive.

The first regular daily motor-buses to compete with the railway appeared in 1920 operated by the National Omnibus & Transport Co; which commenced by offering services from Halstead to Colchester and to the Hedinghams. Several local men soon followed suit, so there was soon competition with one another as well as the railway. Halstead residents could also save themselves a good walk by board-ing the bus near the church at the top of High Street, and also enjoyed a much wider range of departure times and later return times than that offered by the railway. So, the omnibuses prospered and the

Locomotive No. 2, the 0–4–2 ST built by Beyer Peacock (ex-North London Railway) and sold to South Hetton Colliery Co. in 1894 seen here at Haverhill GE station before the platform awnings were provided. The train had just arrived from Chappel.   *Lens of Sutton*

Locomotive No. 2 *Halstead* with five assorted 6-wheelers coaches and the two old straight sided 4-wheelers, awaiting its next duty at Haverhill GE *c.*1900.
                                                          Authors' Collection

CV & H train entering Haverhill GE station behind No. 3 *Colne* in 1911 whilst the GE goods for Cambridge waits in refuge siding. Wagons in the siding on the right are for transfer to or from the CV station. *LCGB Collection*

Locomotive No. 1 with a down train about to pass under Hedingham Road bridge about 1 mile from Halstead. Photographed around 1894 when the locomotive acquired the GE pattern stove-pipe chimney. *Collection A. Smith*

An interesting 1949 scene at Marks Tey Junction. An ex-GE 'Y14' 0–6–0, No. 65473, positioning the Sudbury line train in front with the Colne Valley section in rear. The main line is facing towards Colchester. The signal box formerly located in the vee at the end of the platform is now just beyond the over-line bridge. *John H. Meredith*

A 1954 view showing clearly the Stour/Colne Valley branch platform and up main line platform. British Rail No. 65465 ex-GER Class 'Y14' 0–6–0 is about to leave with the Haverhill (via Colne Valley) train. *P.J. Kelley*

Locomotive No. 5. A splendid picture taken at Haverhill just prior to leaving

An interesting scene at Halstead station of which no particulars have been handed down. It would appear to be a Special comprising a GER private saloon with CV&H goods brake No. 9 attached, about to leave with No. 1 locomotive in charge. At this date the loading dock appears not to have been constructed, and the platform is unpaved. It would seem the event was of more than ordinary importance.   *R.W. Kidner*

Locomotive No. 4 *Hedingham* 2–4–2T shunting in Haverhill (CV) goods yard 1911.   *Authors' Collection*

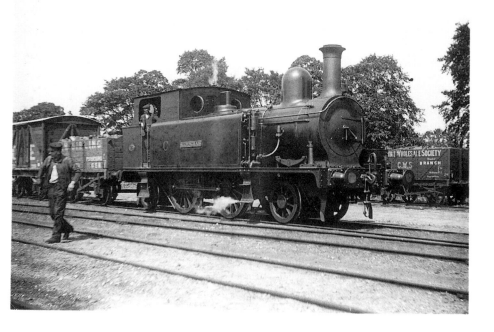

Locomotive No. 3 *Colne* passing Colne Valley Junction *en route* to Chappel. The line to Haverhill CV is on the left. Hamlet Road viaduct is on the right with the signal box just visible behind the engine.   *LCGB Collection*

No. 5 again with an up goods leaving Haverhill with a substantial load for such a small railway. The boiler from locomotive No. 1 is in the last wagon being returned from repairs, *c*.1911.   *LCGB Collection*

Locomotive No. 5 entering Halstead station with an up goods, which includes several trucks of bricks from Purls Hill Siding, *c.*1911.   *LCGB Collection*

No. 62794, BR ex-GE "Intermediate" class 'E4' 2–4–0, at the up platform at Chappel and Wakes Colne with combined Stour Valley line train and the branch train off the Colne Valley. About to start for Marks Tey with an amazing assortment of stock (the third car is a twelve wheeler!).

N.E. Stead Collection

South Hetton Colliery locomotive No. 2, formerly *Hedingham*, on the CV & H
Railway as photographed in 1947, looking rather the worse for wear after 74
years service.   *H. Casserley*

Haverhill (CV) station yard 1911: No. 4 *Hedingham* has just made up the train
and is about to leave for Halstead.   *Authors' Collection*

train gradually lost passengers, and each year the motor-bus came to be regarded by more and more people as the natural method of travel for all local journeys.

Despite the very rural character of the district, the CV & HR was able to enjoy good freight traffics over and above that normally required for supplying the local retailers and agricultural requirements. There was a considerable traffic in raw materials and fuel supplies inward and finished products outward from establishments such as Hunt's Atlas Foundry at Earls Colne, Portway's Tortoise Foundry and Courtauld's Textile Mills in Halstead, Ripper's Joinery Works at Castle Hedingham, Whitlock's at Yeldham who built carts and agricultural machines and Unwin's Seed business at Birdbrook, the several brick yards and a few others.

The appearance of the luxury long-distance motor coach in the late 1920s signalled a further decline in rail passengers. The road from London to Bury St Edmunds was particularly vulnerable because all towns on this route were located on branch or cross-country lines, a point which did not pass unnoticed by the PSV operators both local and from farther afield. By 1929 no less than six different lines of coach were available for a London journey from Halstead with two more joining the route at Braintree. Because of the slow railway journeys the journey-time differential as between rail and road was not very great. Mr Akers who owned the "Bird" coaches at Halstead, Blackwell from Earls Colne, and Chinery who traded as Corona Coaches from Acton near Sudbury all put on services to London this year, and being local could give an earlier first departure time in the morning than those whose service commenced from a distance, so were able to command most of the Halstead area traffic. They all offered a later daily return time than the railway, and there was a theatre service on Saturday nights and a late 10.00 pm trip on Sunday evenings for those spending a week-end in the Metropolis; all new facilities never enjoyed hitherto. Many people looked on these coaches as the height of luxury and every bit as good as riding in a car.

None of these things stirred the railway management to offering anything different even after they had secured a 50% interest in the Eastern National Co., which was the major bus and coach operator in the area.

The outbreak of war in 1939 probably deferred closure of the line by a few years because private motoring almost ceased, the long distance coaches were taken off, bus facilities were restricted but rail traffics, both passenger and freight, increased enormously.

In 1948 the LNER became a part of British Railways, Eastern

Region, which continued without any perceptible change the same service along the valley, and the inexorable decline in all traffic continued unabated as more and more people turned to private road travel with all its well known advantages. By the 1950s this trend was beginning to affect the bus companies also which, during and after the war, had enjoyed an unprecedented bonanza, but were now beginning to feel the draught.

Freight traffic was now also diminishing rapidly, mainly of course because of the door-to-door facilities which road transport offered, which the railway could not do much about. There were other factors such as the former extensive milk traffic which was now collected direct at the farm, more factories and warehouse distributors were employing their own transport. North Sea Gas closed down all the local gas-works and the greater use of electrical equipment steadily reduced domestic coal requirements etc.

One would have expected the introduction of diesel haulage when there was a complete recasting of the timetables for the Colne Valley line and the associated lines to Cambridge, Sudbury and Bury St Edmunds provided the opportunity to bring in some long wanted service improvements. Not so. Apart from two or three additional trains down to Sudbury, the service on the Colne Valley was even more dreadful. The first Up train, normally the most important of the day, now entailed a thirty minute wait at Marks Tey for the London connection; the next required two changes of carriage, as did the third, whilst the fourth and last needed two and a half hours to reach Liverpool Street. In the Down direction the fortuitous operation of a positioning movement enabled the early 6.54 am departure to now arrive at Halstead at 8.37 am, the fastest ever recorded! The second Down train required two changes, the third took about two hours for the trip, the fourth Down took *three hours*. The final train was rather faster but left no later than 5.45 (5.30 on Saturdays), the passenger reaching Halstead by 7.26 pm. It makes one wonder if they were trying to ensure that nobody used the service, so that it could be closed down sooner.

Local traffic along the valley had long since found other ways of getting around, and those requiring to make long distance journeys would take themselves or be taken to the nearest main-line station where they could board a fast train.

By 1961 the decision had been taken to withdraw all passenger facilities from the Colne Valley and the associated branches at the end of the year. A replacement omnibus service was provided by arrangement with Eastern National, but very few used it, in fact so few, that, after two years and the need for a heavy subsidy, it was taken off. It does seem remarkable that the road facilities provided after a rail closure were consistently not mentioned in the railway timetables or any combined through booking arrangements provided.

A few other matters concerning the line whilst it was in the hands of the LNER and BR remain to be recorded. As the Colne Valley and Halstead Company's locomotives were withdrawn, the replacements were always – except at the very last – of Great Eastern origin, and usually tender types, which were now wearing the new overall black livery which enjoyed a red lining-out until about 1928 when it became an unrelieved black, drawing ex-GER coaching stock now in process of changing from deep crimson with the rather splendid GER armorial device on the sides and the very large numerals designating the class of accommodation on the doors, to the varnished teak finish (ex-GNR) now favoured. They were generally somewhat elderly gaslit six-wheelers, sometimes with clerestory roofs. Many were composites of which there were several variations. Third interiors were upholstered in red plush, and firsts in blue, and all carried in the centre of the partitions above the cushioning a fine coloured map of the system including a picture of a "Claud Hamilton" in royal blue, one of the Continental steamships and a GER scarlet motor bus; these were flanked by photographs of places of interest or beauty spots by Payne Jennings, some of which could still be seen in the 1950s. In later years as more of the new standard Gresley pattern bogie-stock became available for main-line trains, the displaced GE corridor stock with the small end vestibules gradually found its way to the country branches until diesel railcars or multiple units finally took over. During the war and post-war years much of this old carriage stock was painted in an overall dull brown shade.

Of the locomotive stock used, the well known and long lived ex-GE 'Y14' – 'J15' in LNER parlance; 0–6–0 tender engines, the "maids of all work" handled all the traffic for most of the time. Five of them were equipped with side-window cabs and tender-cabs for running tender first there being no turntable at either of the Haverhill stations. From time to time they might be replaced by an ex-GE 'T26'/'E4' 2–4–0 "Intermediate" some of which also had been fitted with tender-cabs, more usually on a through working from Cambridge where several were always stationed. Through excursions from Cambridge and beyond going to Clacton-on-Sea or to Walton-on-Naze were usually routed over the Colne Valley Line on Sundays on which day it was always open. These could be hauled by a "Claud Hamilton" 4–4–0 or a rebuilt ex-GE 'T19' "Express" 2–4–0 now 4–4–0 class 'D13', the very last one of the class was working on this line until finally withdrawn c.1943/4. Immediately prior to the introduction of diesel power some Ivatt class 2MT 2–6–0 tender locomotives came on the scene. Diesel shunters handled the remaining freight traffic until the final closure.

Apart from the alterations at Halstead and Haverhill South which have already been mentioned, the whole of the station premises remained "Colne Valley" until the end. Certain signals were replaced when necessary by some of GE pattern, and under BR the new design standard style name boards were attached to the station lamp standards and name plates on doors and notice boards. The LNER fitted some station name plates of GE pattern cast-iron to platform seat-back rests.

One accident of an almost identical nature to the discreditable affair at Parsonage Lane, Halstead, occurred shortly after the last war at Yeldham station. The Down morning goods had just completed shunting the yard using the long dead-end siding parallel to the running line at the Haverhill end of the station as a shunting neck. The driver backed the rest of wagons (drawn out of the yard) onto the remainder of the train which had been left standing at the platform, but did not observe that he had not backed far enough to clear the switch leading into the running line. The guard, having consulted his watch, said "Time we were off", and walked back towards his brake van expecting the driver would set back enough to clear the point which the signalman could not alter, nor could he lower the starting signal whilst the engine stood on it. Instead, the driver "blew up" and put on steam without a glance at the starter – neither did the fireman, and off they went down the long siding. All on the platform shouted as loudly as possible, the guard screwed down his brake and blew his whistle vigorously and hopped off onto the platform, and all waited for the inevitable. The train, at increasing speed, carried away the stops at the end and dropped into soft ground which quickly brought it to a halt, remaining upright fortuitously. Luckily neither of the crew took any harm from the tender or its appurtenances when it dipped downward, though it was holed by the draw-hook of a heavy parcel van next to it.

The LNER continued during its lifetime to display GE pattern time-tables which continued under BR for some years, but were replaced later by train departure lists only, so that no passenger could ascertain return times without recourse to the enquiry or booking office.

Although its days were fast drawing to a close, the Colne Valley did just succeed in attaining its centenary on 16th April, 1960, though there was not much to celebrate.

The last passenger "special" to make use of the line would appear to have been a "Rambler's Special" which took place on Sunday, 8th

October of that year: it came from Liverpool Street via Bartlow and Haverhill to Halstead, and then continued privately to Chappel & Wakes Colne and then to Marks Tey with halts as required for photographic purposes.

The final obsequies (so far as passenger operations were concerned) took place with little ostentation on the evening of the last Saturday in December 1961, when the very last passenger train ran over the length of the line to Haverhill. The occasion was admirably described by Eric Axton in his excellent little book *The History of Public Transport in the Halstead Area*, from which the following extracts have been taken by kind permission:

. . .(At Marks Tey) . . . the passengers were made up of about twenty "enthusiasts" bidding the line a last farewell, and a few other passengers that enthusiasts call "naturals". . . . The journey from Marks Tey to Chappel was uneventful as this part of the line was not closing but here we turned on to the doomed Colne Valley line and soon came to Boley Road crossing where the door of the crossing cottage stood open and a little group of people stood in the light streaming out and gave us a wave and a cheer as we ran through. At the first stop at White Colne an elderly lady alighted and disappeared into the darkness shopping bag in hand. The stationman waved us off. At Earls Colne our arrival and departure caused no stir, then we ran into Halstead to the accompaniment of exploding detonators. A good number of people were assembled on the platform and there was considerable coming and going, and as we pulled away the signalman came out on the balcony of the Trinity Street Signal Box and waved us past. Hedingham had its little group to say farewell as had Yeldham. At Birdbrook, nobody, here while we stopped the enthusiasts photographed the stationman who told them he was being transferred to Sturmer. So far, at the previous stations there would still be a goods train but for Birdbrook it was the last train ever. Reaching Haverhill North we all alighted: somehow there was nothing to say.

The weather played its part, the night produced a blizzard, and for the next two days rail and bus services were dislocated. A fitting farewell.

Freight traffic continued to be handled for a little longer. After the cessation of passenger trains the Yeldham–Birdbrook–Colne Valley Junction section closed entirely. Freight for Haverhill South was worked round by shunter trips from Haverhill North, and traffic for points Chappel to Yeldham was worked from that end. At the close of 1964 Yeldham and Castle & Sible Hedingham both lost their goods services. The two remaining sections, e.g. Chappel–Halstead and Haverhill North to South, lingered on until April 1965 when they shared the same fate, which is recorded thus by Eric Axton:

. . . the line finally died on Maundy Thursday 1965 when the last goods train in service pulled out of Halstead at half-past three on a grey afternoon. Three people watched as the diesel-shunter with two box wagons and some empty coal trucks gave a last mournful wail on its hooter and drew slowly away. As it rolled away Halstead heard for the last time the sound of metal wheels on metal rails.

I was unable to be present . . . but I was near enough to hear that last whistle and the wheels rolling away down the valley.

Epilogue

It is hard to realise that almost a quarter of a century has passed since the sound of a train could be heard passing along the valley. Before, therefore, finally closing this account of the line, let us go over the way it once went, and note what has taken place since.

Commencing once again, where it all began at "Chappel and Wakes Colne for the Colne Valley Line" to give it its full title, for though trains still call at the station, the second half of the title is no longer appropriate.

Here a more cheerful note may be struck. It is still a place of railway activity where the sound of safety valves blowing off, the sight of smoke and the smell of hot oil and burning fuel can still be savoured. Here we are at the headquarters of the Stour Valley Railway Preservation Society formed by a group of steam enthusiasts who feared that BR would be withdrawing all railway operations from the Stour Valley. Determined that some part of the line should be saved, the Society was brought into being, and has succeeded in acquiring the goods yard and station buildings at Chappel where a number of locomotives and other items of rolling stock and railway equipment can be seen.

BR however is still operating a service of trains between Marks Tey and Sudbury which still call at the Down platform. If this service should be withdrawn in the future, the SVPS is now in a strong position to operate a service. Meanwhile it is limited to steam working within the confines of the old goods yard.

The steel footbridge connecting the platforms, and the waiting and other rooms that were on the Up platform are no longer there, though the platform itself remains. The Down side buildings are still extant and serve as tea-room, book and souvenir shop and offices and stores for the Society.

Continuing along the line little now remains to remind us of the previous existence of a railway through the valley. At White Colne the station building has become a private residence, a vestige of the former platform remains and the goods yard now serves as a depot for lorries. Much of the formation can be followed without too much difficulty except in those places where the track becomes level with the adjoining farmland into which it has been absorbed. Underline bridges have all been removed. Earls Colne station has been occupied by a light engineering business and Hunt's Engineering Works is happily still in action.

Continuing on to Halstead it is hard indeed to realise that here was once the headquarter organisation, works and running department of a railway company. All has been demolished. A medical centre, groups of flats, sundry small industrial or warehouse units and two super-stores have now covered the site and a part of the adjoining Courtauld property, and the old Tortoise Foundry now defunct. The station forecourt now serves as an omnibus standing.

At the Hedinghams the two underline bridges have gone, also the gas works, but Rippers' works is now a part of the Bowater group. The formation may still be seen to Nunnery Lane, where now is another centre of preservation activity. In 1974 a band of enthusiasts and preservationists got together to try and save something of the former CV & H and succeeded in forming a new Colne Valley Railway Company Limited which now owns about one and a half miles of permanent way on which preserved engines and other items may be seen in operation on steam days.[1] Going forward to Yeldham and Birdbrook virtually nothing now remains. At Haverhill (CV) it is possible to recognise something of its former use among the sundry small occupiers.

Anyone entering Haverhill from the east cannot possibly miss the Hamlet Road Viaduct with its three very large arches, which carried the connecting link across from the CV to the GE line, which although GE property was only used by CV trains. It is now the subject of a preservation order and so forms a permanent reminder to later generations that hereabouts was once a steam railway as it sits astride the main road looking very solid indeed. It can also serve as a fitting memorial to the memory of those few public spirited citizens who strove so hard and found so much money (for which they received little return or recognition) to ensure the railway came up the valley, and afterwards ensured that it continued to operate when at times the odds against it seemed hopeless.

---

[1] *See Appendix F.*

Appendix A

The Colne Valley and Halstead Railway Arrangements Act, 1885. (48 and 49 Vic. Cap. 194).

SUMMARY OF PROVISIONS:
1. The Receivership to be terminated.
2. An Arbitrator was to be appointed to decide the constitution of the Board, and the mode of governing the Company.
3. All unissued stock under previous Acts, and the £60,000 of shares held as collateral security by Mr Brewster and Mr Tweedy were to be extinguished.
4. The Company were authorized to borrow a sum not exceeding £36,000 and any further sum authorized by the Arbitrator on mortgage of their undertaking, providing the total so raised did not exceed £50,000 in all.
5. Deposits on future Bills were not to be paid out of capital.

SUMMARY OF AWARDS OF ARBITRATOR:
1. Preliminary Award (November 1885).
   The Board to consist of six Directors, three to be appointed by the holders of Statutory and Construction Bonds and by the Judgment Creditors, and three to be appointed by the Preference and Ordinary Shareholders.
2. Final Award.
   (a) The Company was empowered to raise £14,000 on mortgage of the undertaking in addition to the sum of £36,000 laid down in the Act, making £50,000 in all, such mortgage debentures or debenture stock to be called "A" debentures or debenture stock.
   (b) Creditors on Statutory Bonds, Construction Bonds, and Judgment Creditors were to rank on an equality and receive debentures to be called "B" debenture stock in satisfaction and in lieu of all their previous rights and claims. (A schedule was annexed showing the amounts of these debts.)
   (c) The method of payment of interest was as follows: No dividend was to be paid to shareholders until 1% had been paid to "B" Debenture Holders. Any sum left over after this had been done was to be divided so that Preference Shareholders should receive twice as much as Ordinary Shareholders and "B" Debenture holders twice as much as the Preference Shareholders. However, the "B" Debenture Holders should not receive more than 4%, and any balance after that was to be divided so that Preference Shareholders received twice as much as Ordinary Shareholders until the amount paid on Preference shares reached 5% when any further balance should go to the Ordinary Shareholders.
   (d) The costs of the Arbitration were to be paid out of borrowings.

Appendix B

Terms of Absorption of the Colne Valley and Halstead Railway into the London and North Eastern Railway, 1923.

Holders of Colne Valley 5% "A" debentures received £125 4% LNER First Preference stock in exchange for each £100 of Colne Valley stock held.

Holders of Colne Valley 4% "B" debentures received £10 LNER 5% Preferred Ordinary stock for each £100 of Colne Valley stock held.

Holders of Colne Valley Preference and Ordinary shares received £1 10s. 0d. and £1 5s. 0d. respectively for each £100 of Colne Valley stock held.

Appendix C

Early Timetables

January 1861

		Weekdays				Sundays	
UP		a.m.	p.m.	p.m.	p.m.	a.m.	p.m.
Halstead .... dep		8.25	12.35	4.05	6.25	8.50	4.55
Colne (White Colne)		8.35	*	*	*	9.03	5.08
Chappel .... arr.		8.43	12.55	4.25	6.40	9.10	5.15
DOWN							
Chappel .... dep.		10.15	1.40	6.05	7.50	10.00	6.55
Colne .... „		10.20	1.45	*	8.00	10.10	7.05
Halstead .... arr.		10.40	2.00	6.20	8.10	10.25	7.20

* Calls if required.

July 1861 (i.e. immediately after the opening to Castle Hedingham). The times at Halstead, Colne and Chappel remained the same, but trains were allowed 15 minutes for the run between Halstead and Castle Hedingham both Up and Down, with the exception of the evening Up which ran 35 minutes later, and the Sunday morning Down which was retarded 5 minutes.

September 1861

Additional trains ran as follows:

		a.m.	a.m.	p.m.
Halstead .... dep.		7.40W	8.00S	2.30S
Castle Hedingham .... arr.		7.55W	8.15S	2.45S

		p.m.	a.m.	p.m.
Castle Hedingham ... dep.		8.35W	11.00S	8.00S
Halstead .... arr.		8.50W	11.15S	8.15S

W – Weekdays   S – Sundays

November 1862 (i.e. immediately after the opening to Yeldham) The same service as appeared in the September 1861 timetable was used, with a further 10 minutes running time added. There was a slight alteration to

89

the running times of the Up evening train, and last Up "short" train to Halstead.

June 1863
On the opening of the last section of the line to Haverhill, the following timetable was introduced:

UP	Weekdays				Sundays	
	a.m.	a.m.	p.m.	p.m.	a.m.	p.m.
Haverhill .... dep.	7.45	8.15	11.55	3.20	5.30	8.05	4.10
Yeldham .... „	8.05	8.35	12.13	3.40	5.50	8.25	4.30
Hedingham ... „	8.12	8.42	12.20	3.50	6.00	8.35	4.40
Halstead .... „	8.25	8.55	12.35	4.05	6.23	8.50	4.55
Colne .... „	8.37	9.07	*	*	6.36	9.03	5.08
Chappel ...... arr.	8.43	9.15	12.55	4.25	6.43	9.10	5.15

DOWN							
Chappel ..... dep.	9.30	10.15	1.40	6.50	7.50	10.05	6.55
Colne .... „	9.40	10.23	1.45	6.10	7.55	10.13	7.03
Halstead .... „	10.00	10.40	2.00	6.13	8.10	10.30	7.20
Hedingham ... „	10.15	10.50	2.10	6.30	8.20	10.40	7.30
Yeldham .... „	10.30	10.57	2.20	6.40	8.30	10.50	7.40
Haverhill ..... arr.	10.50	11.17	2.40	7.00	8.50	11.10	8.00

* Calls when required.

GREAT EASTERN RAILWAY TIME TABLE

SUDBURY BRANCH — FRIDAY, July 1, 1864.

Week Days. | Sundays

FROM	1 and 2 Parl. Morn.	1 and 2 class. Even.		1 and 2 Exps. Even.	1, 2, 3 class. Even.	1, 2, 3 cla. P. Morn.	1, 2, 3 class. Eve
Colchester	9.25	....	...	5.25	6.45	9.35	5.30
Marks Tey	10. 0	1.25	...	5.52	7.35	9.50	6.40
Chappel	10.10	1.35	...	6. 2	7.45	10. 0	6.50
Colne	10.23	1.45	...	6.10	7.55	10.13	7. 0
Halstead ...	10.40	1.58	...	6.20	8. 8	10.30	7.13
C.Hedingham	10.50	2. 8	...	6.30	8.18	10.40	7.23
Yeldham ...	10.57	2.18	...	6.35	8.23	10.50	7.28
Birdbrook ...	11 10	2.32	...	6.55	8.42	11.10	7.50
Haverhill ..	11.17	2.40	...	7. 0	8.50	11.15	8. 0
Bures	10.20	†	...	†	†	10. 8	7. 0
Sudbury	10.35	1.55	...	6.20	3. 5	10.20	7.15

(*Colne Valley Company.*)

FROM	1 and 2 Exps. Morn.	1, 2, 3 Parl. Morn.	T.S. 1, 2 cl. Even.	1 and 2 class. Even.	1, 2, 3 class. Even.	1, 2, 3 cla. P. Morn.	1, 2, 3 class. Eve
Sudbury	8.30	8.55	12.40	4.15	6.25	8.55	5. 0
Bures	†	9. 5	†	†	†	9. 7	5.12
Haverhill ...	7.55	8.15	11.55	3.15	5.25	8. 0	4. 0
Birdbrook ...	†	8.22	12. 3	3.23	5.33	8. 5	4. 5
Yeldham ...	8.15	8.33	12.22	3.42	5.52	8.25	4.25
C.Hedingham	†	8.42	12.27	3.47	6. 0	8.35	4.35
Halstead ...	8.30	8.55	12.37	4. 0	6.20	8.50	4.50
Colne	†	9. 7	12.50	4.10	6 32	9. 3	5. 3
Chappel	8.48	9.20	1. 0	4.31	6.45	9.17	5.22
Marks Tey	8.57	9.30	1.10	4.42	6.55	9.28	5.35
Colchester	...	10. 4	1.32	4.55	7.45	9.50	5.47

(*Colne Valley Company.*)

† Will call at these stations to take up and set down passengers.

Return Tickets at Single Fares are issued every Sunday by all Trains to and from all Stations on the Eastern Union division, available on the day of issue only.

T.S.—SUDBURY AND COLCHESTER MARKET DAYS.—On Thursday and Saturdays the 12.40 p.m. Train from Sudbury will start at 12 noon, and run through to Colchester ; returning from Colchester to Sudbury at 1 0 p.m., calling at the intermediate Stations. 1st, 2nd and 3rd Class.

Part of timetable of GE and other railways which appeared in the *Essex & West Suffolk* newspaper on 1st July, 1864, before provision of station at White Colne, showing former name of Earls Colne station.

The Guard will be held responsible for examining at each station all Coaches and Waggons, and must see that the Doors and Sheets are properly secured, also that the couplings are safe before the train starts.

The Guards and Drivers are cautioned against allowing unauthorised persons to ride in Brake or on Engine. It is the duty of the Guard to report any irregularity or unusual occurrence on the Road.

TAIL LAMPS AND BOARDS.—A Tail Lamp to be carried by day and lighted Tail Lamp by night. Or when there is a special or Excursion Train to follow, a "Train Following Board" by day or extra lighted Tail Lamp by night must be hung behind. The Guard is to carry Side and Tail Lamps, and is responsible for these instructions being strictly carried out.

HAND FLAGS AND FOG SIGNALS.—Each Ganger to be supplied with a set of flags and fog signals to be used as set forth in Books of Rules and Regulations supplied to each servant of the company.

COLLECTION AND EXAMINATION OF TICKETS.—All Trains to be examined at Earls Colne and Birdbrook. Tickets to be collected where the Passengers alight, except Haverhill Tickets which must be collected and cancelled at Birdbrook.

The staff are at all times to be prepared for the passing of Special Trains, which may be run without notice, and the Line must be kept clear.

Platelayers are cautioned to keep a good look out when using Trollies.

A revised book of Rules and Regulations approved by the Board of Directors on 1st January, 1916, has been issued to the staff, and a copy of the Book must be in possession of each Servant of the Company when on duty.

ELIOT S. HAWKINS,
General Manager.

Private—For the use of the Company's Servants only

COLNE VALLEY RAILWAY.

From APRIL 9th, 1923,
(UNTIL FURTHER NOTICE.)

WORKING TIME TABLES
OF
PASSENGER AND GOODS TRAINS.

Each Officer and Servant of the Company who is supplied with a copy of the Working Time Tables will be held responsible for reading carefully and obeying all the Regulations and Instructions contained therein so far as he is personally concerned.

The Station Masters must Personally see that the Staff connected with the Traffic Department are supplied with a Copy of each issue.

The Permanent Way Inspector, and the Locomotive Foreman will also see that the Staff, connected with their respective departments be supplied with a Copy of each issue.

DOWN TRAINS.

Week Days. | Sundays.

Miles from Chappel	FROM		2	4	6	8	10	12	14	16	18	20	22	24	26	28	30	32	34	2	4	6	8
			L.E.	Cars	Gds	Cars	Gds.	Pass	Pass.	Gds.	Gds.	Gds.	Gds	Gds	Gds.	Pass.	Pass.	Gds	Gds	Cars	Pass	L.E.	L.E.	P.
			a.m.	a.m.	a.m.	a.m.	a.m.	a.m.	a.m.	a.m.	p.m.	p.m.	p.m	p.m.	p.m.	p.m.	p.m.	p.m.	p.m	p.m	a.m.	a.m.	a.m.	p.m.	
	Chappel	dep.		6 20				9 26	11 33		2 5					4 5	7 17	6 5	8 0	11 0			
2½	White Colne	ar.		6 25				9 30	11 37		2 12					4 9	7 21	6 10	8 5	11 4			
		dep.		6 26				9 31	11 38		2 17					4 10	7 22	6 13	8 8	11 5			
3½	Earls Colne	ar.		6 35				9 34	11 41		2 22					4 13	7 25	6 17	8 12	11 8			
		dep.		6 50				9 35	11 42		2 45					4 14	7 28	6 27	8 25	11 9			
6	Halstead	ar.		6 56				9 41	11 48		2 50					4 20	7 32	6 30	8 30	11 15			
		dep.	6 45			7 30		9 43	11 50		3 20	1 40				4 22	7 34	stop	stop	11 17			
9	Hedingham	ar.	6 53			7 38		9 50	11 54		3 30	1 48				4 29	7 41			11 24			
		dep.	6 55		8 10				11 57		3 40	2 0				4 30	7 43			11 25			
12	Yeldham	ar.			8 18				12 2		3 48	2 9				4 36	7 48			11 31			
		dep.			8 30				12 3		4 0	2 13				4 37	7 49			11 32			
15½	Birdbrook	ar.			8 40				12 12		4 10	2 30				4 46	7 57			11 41			
		dep.			8 52				12 14		4 20	2 35				4 48	8 0			11 43			
18	Colne Valley Jct.				8 58		9 10	9 35	12 19	12 36	1 41	4 25	2 40	3 5	4 50	4 53	8 5			8 32	11 48	12 8	5 49	
	Haverhill G.E. ar.		7 20				9 12	9 40	12 22	1 42	4 30	2 45			4 56				8 35	11 51		5 51	
	Haverhill C.V. ar.		7 25			9 0				12 38		3 7	4 55				3 8			12 11			8	
			M.S.	M.							N.S.	S.	S.	N.S.			S.			N S			

The Sunday Trains commence running 3rd June.

UP TRAINS.

Week Days. | Sundays.

Miles from Haverhill	FROM	1	3	5	7	9	11	13	15	17	19	21	23	25	27	29	1	3	5	7	9
		Gds.	Pass.	Pass.	Cars.	Pass.	Gds	Gds.	Gds	Gds.	Pass.	Gds	Gds.	Gds.	Gds.	Pass.	Cars.	Pass	L.E.	L.E.	Pass
		a.m.	a.m.	a.m.	a.m.	a.m.	a.m.	a.m.	am	p.m	p.m.	p.m.	p.m.	p.m.	p.m	p m	p.m.	a.m.	a.m.	a.m.	p.m.	p.m.
	Haverhill C.V. dep.				7 38	9 29		10 15	12 31		2 0	4 45		3 0		6 8		8 11	12 5		5 58	
	Haverhill G.E. dep.				7 40	9 31	9 34	10 20	12 35	1 43	2 2	4 49	5 18	3 5	6 10	8 31	8 16	7	5 48	6 5	
1	Colne Valley Jct. ar.				7 45	9 36		10 27			2 8		5 25			6 14		8 19			6 7	
3½	Birdbrook ar.				7 47	9 38		10 35			2 9		5 35			6 17		8 53			6 7	
	dep.				7 55	9 46		10 55			2 17		5 43			6 25		9 0			6 16	
7	Yeldham ar.				7 56	9 47		11 20			2 18		5 47			6 26		9 7			6 21	
	dep.			8 2	9 53		11 28			2 24		6 0			6 32		9 9			6 24	
9½	Hedingham ar.			8 3	8 3	9 54		12 0			2 25		6 8			6 33		9 16			6 30	
13	Halstead dep.			8 10	8 10	10 1		12 10			2 34		6 20			6 40		9 18			6 36	
	dep.	5 30	8 12	8 12	10 3		1 0			2 54		6 56			6 44		9 21			6 40	
15½	Earls Colne dep.	5 38	8 18	8 18	10 10		1 10			2 40		7 0			5 49		9 24			6 43	
	dep.	5 45	8 20	8 20	10 11		1 25			2 43		7 25			5 50	6 50	9 26			6 45	
17½	White Colne dep.	5 49	8 23	8 23	10 13		1 30			2 46		7 30			5 55	6 52	9 28			6 48	
	dep.	5 55	8 25	8 25	10 16		1 40			2 47		7 35			5 40	6 54	9 31			6 15	
19	Chappel ar.	6 3	8 30	8 30	10 21		1 48			2 52		7 43			5 48	7 0	9 36			6 20	
		N.M.	M.							N.S.	N.S.	S.		S.							

The Sunday Trains commence running 3rd June.

Week Day Trains.——Notes.

The figures under which a bar (thus ———) is placed show where Trains from opposite directions are appointed to cross each other, or allow following trains to pass.

Trains between Chappel and Earls Colne will be worked under the Electric Train Staff Block Telegraph [Regulation

M.—Mondays only.   N.S.—Not Saturdays.

N.M.—Not Mondays.   S.—Saturdays only.

M S   Tuesday to Saturday inclusive, leave Halstead 7.40 a.m., arrive Hedingham 7.48.

The last Working Timetable to be issued by the CV&H Railway 9th April, 1923.

COLNE VALLEY TRAINS DEPARTING FROM CHAPPEL (G. E.) & ARRIVING AT HAVERHILL (G. E.) STATIONS.

Week Days. **Sundays**

FROM	1	2	3	4	5	6	7	8	9	10	11	12	13	14	15	16	17	18	19	20	21	22
	Gds	A Car	Pas	Car	B Gds	A Pas			Pas	B Pas	Gds	Gds	B Gds	Pas	B Pas	Pas.	B Gds.	Mid		Car	Pas	Eng
	a.m.	a.m.	a.m.	a.m.	a.m.	a.m.			a.m.	p.m.	p.m.	p.m	p.m.	p.m.	p.m.	p.m	p.m.	p.m.		a.m.	a.m.	p.m.
Chappel ......dep.	8 30	...	9 18	...	...	...	—		1128	1 13	...	1 26	1 43	1 15	3 5	7 1	8 0	9 2		...	1055	...
Haverhill ...arr.	......	7 25	...	9 33	10 0	1025			1218	1 33	4 30	4 35	5 10	8 58	7 49					8 45	1140	5 12

A Mondays and Saturdays only.   **B** Saturdays only.   **C** Not on Mondays and Saturdays.

COLNE VALLEY TRAINS DEPARTING FROM HAVERHILL (G. E.) AND ARRIVING AT CHAPPEL (G. E.) STATIONS.

Week Days. **Sundays.**

FROM	1	2	3	4	5	6	7	8	9	10	11	12	13	14	15	16	17	18	19	20	21	22	23	24
	A Gd	Pas	Pas	Pas	Gds	C Pas	B Gds	Gds	Gds	Gds	Pas	C Gds	Gds	Gds	Pas	C Cr	Gds	Car	B Gds	D Pas	En.		M	
	a.m	a.m	a.m.	a.m.	a.m.	a.m.	a.m.	p.m.	p.m.	p.m.	p.m.	p.m.	p.m.	p.m.	p.m.	p.m	p.m	p.m.	p.m.	a.m.	a.m.	p.m.		
Haverhill dep.	......	736	...	9 43	11 0	1125	1140	1245	8 30	...	2 36	4 50	...	5 15	8 19	7 0	...	7 52	...	7 58	8 48	1145	5 13	
Chappel ...arr.	543	...	8 30	1039	1 54	1220	...	...	...	2 33	3 27	...	5 49	...	6 40	...	7 49	...	8 30	8 50	9 40	...	6 13	

Mondays and Saturdays only.   **B** Not Mondays and Saturdays.   **C** Saturdays only.   **D** Not Saturdays.

Extract from Great Eastern working timetable of 1913: the number of CV goods arrivals and departures at Haverhill (GE) is indicative of the quantity of freight traffic exchanged here: most will be trip trains between the two stations.

Norwich, Mark's Tey and Haverhill (Colne Valley Line)

		WEEKDAYS											SUNDAYS			
		a.m.	a.m.	a.m.	a.m.	a.m.	a.m.	p.m.	p.m.	p.m.	a.m.	a.m.	p.m.	p.m.	p.m.	
Norwich (Thorpe) ... dep.		...	...	...	...	8 50	...	1022	...	3 44	...	...	...	...	...	
Ipswich ... ,,	7 55	...	...	...	1027	...	2 5	...	5 52	9 55	...	6 20	...	...		
Colchester ... ,,	...	8 45	...	...	11 5	...	3 30	...	6 46	1035	...	8 25	...	...		
Mark's Tey ... arr.	8 45	8 57	...	...	1118	...	3 40	...	6 56	1049	...	8 35	...	...		
London (Liverpool St.) dep.	...	6 50	...	...	10 3	...	2 15	...	5 42	9 15	...	...	...	4 40	
Mark's Tey ... ,,	...	9 13	...	...	1124	...	3 52	...	7 4	1055	...	...	...	8 42	
Chappel & Wakes Colne arr.	...	9 22	...	...	1132	...	4 2	...	7 13	11 4	...	..	...	8 51	
Chappel & Wakes Colne dep.	...	9 26	...	...	1136	...	4 6	...	7 18	11 8	...	...	...	8 55	
White Colne ... ,,	...	9 32	...	...	1142	...	4 12	...	7 24	1114	...	...	...	9 1	
Earls Colne ... ,,	...	9 36	...	...	1146	...	4 16	...	7 28	1118	...	...	...	9 5	
Halstead ... ,,	...	9 44	...	...	1154	...	4 24	...	7 36	1126	...	...	...	9 13	
Sible & Castle Hed'gham ,,	...	9 50	...	...	12 1	...	4 31	...	7 43	1133	...	...	...	9 20	
Yeldham ... ,,	...	...	...	...	12 7	...	4 37	...	7 49	1139	...	...	...	9 26	
Birdbrook ... ,,	...	...	...	·...	1215	...	4 45	...	7 57	1147	...	...	...	9 34	
Haverhill (North) ... arr.	...	...	...	...	1223	...	4 55	...	8 7	1157	...	...	...	9 44	
Haverhill (North) ... dep.	7†58	...	9 29	...	2 0	...	6 6	...	...	8 40	...	5 54	...			
Birdbrook ... ,,	7†47	...	9 38	...	2 9	...	6 15	...	...	8 49	...	6 3	...			
Yeldham ... ,,	7 55	...	9 46	...	2 17	...	6 23	...	...	8 57	...	6 11	...			
Sible & Castle Hed'gham ,,	8 1	...	9 52	...	2 23	...	6 29	...	...	9 3	...	6 17	...			
Halstead ... ,,	8 12	...	10 3	...	2 34	...	6 40	...	...	9 14	...	6 28	...			
Earls Colne ... ,,	8 19	...	1010	...	2 41	...	6 47	...	...	9 20	...	6 35	...			
White Colne ... ,,	8 23	...	1014	...	2 45	...	6 51	...	...	9 24	...	6 39	...			
Chappel & Wakes Colne arr.	8 29	...	1020	...	2 51	...	6 57	...	...	9 30	...	6 45	...			
Chappel & Wakes Colne dep	8 35	...	1026	...	2 57	...	7 12	...	...	9 37	...	6 54	...			
Mark's Tey ... arr.	8 42	...	1033	...	3 4	...	7 19	...	...	9 44	...	7 1	...			
London (Liverpool St.) ,,	9 54	...	1143	...	4 58	...	9 17	...	...	1143	...	9 3	...			
Mark's Tey ... dep.	8 50	...	1035	...	3 6	...	7 28	...	...	9 48	...	7 5	...			
Colchester ... arr.	8 59	...	1044	...	3 15	...	7 38	...	...	9 57	...	7 14	...			
Ipswich ... ,,	9 41	...	1148	...	4†50	...	8§39	...	...	1049	...	9 47	...			
Norwich (Thorpe) ... ,,	1117	...	2 0	...	5 45	...	...	...	...	1 17	...	...	...			

† Mons. only.   ‡ On Sats. arrive Ipswich 4.4 p.m.   § On Sats. arrive Ipswich 9.35 p.m.
* Via Colchester.

A page from the "Business Man's Timetable" for July 1927, a Norwich publication, showing all important connections: compare with LNER timetable on the next page.

CHAPPEL AND WAKES COLNE and HAVERHILL (North).

Miles	Down.	Week Days.		Suns.	Miles	Up.	Week Days.		Suns.
		mrn|mrn	aft|aft| S	mrn| aft.			mrn|mrn	aft|aft| S	mrn| aft
	London (L'pool St.) dep.	6 55|10 3	215|6 42|7 42	9 36|6 45		Haverhill (North) ...dep.	7 41|9 31	2 26 12|8 35	8 40|6 2
—	Chappel **1** ....dep.	9 25|1156	..	4 57 2|9 34	1110|8 12	3	Birdbrook	7 49|9 39	2 10|6 20|8 43	8 48|6 11
2	White Colne	9 31|1141	..	4107 25|9 38	1115|8 18	7	Yeldham	7 56|9 46	2 17|6 24|850	8 56|6 22
3½	Earls Colne	9 35|1145	..	4147 29|9 42	1119|8 22	10	Sible & Castle Hedingham	8 3|9 53	2 24|6 35|856	9 1|6 25
6	Halstead...............	9 43|1152	..	4217 36|9 49	1126|8 29	13	Halstead	8 11|10 42	31|6 44|9 3	9 9|6 37
9	Sible & Castle Hedingham	9 50|1159	..	4287 43 9 56	11338 36	15½	Earls Colne	8 17|1010	2 37|6 50|9 9	9 15|6 44
12	Yeldham...............	10 0|12 4	..	4337 48|10 1	11388 42	17	White Colne............	8 20|1013	2 40|6 53|912	9 18|6 45
16	Birdbrook	10 8|1212	..	4417 56|10 9	11468 50	19	Chappel **1** (above) ..arr.	8 27|1018	2 45|6 58|917	9 23|6 51
19	Haverhill (N.) (above) arr.	1016 12.20	..	4498 4|1017	11548 58	69½	London (L'pool St.) arr.	9 56|1140	4 57|9 18	..	11 22|8 3

1 Chappel and Wakes Colne   **S** Sats. only

LNER timetable for Colne Valley line of March 1938 which only shows the London connection as shown in "Bradshaw" and the LNER's own timetables.

Table 26   CHAPPEL AND WAKES COLNE, HALSTEAD and HAVERHILL

Miles		Week Days										Sundays	
		am			am			pm			pm		pm
25	London (L'pool St) dep	6 54	..	..	1036	..	..	2×27	..	..	4 56	..	4 45	..	..
—	Chappel & Wakes C. dep	9 14			12 9			4 46			6 34		6 35	
2	White Colne _ _	9 19			1214			4 51			6 39		6 40	
3½	Earls Colne _ _ _ _	9 23			1218			4 55			6 43		6 44	
6	Halstead	9 31			1225			5b 4			6 58		6 51	
9½	Sible and Castle Hedingham	9z46			1232			5 12			7 6		6 58	
12	Yeldham _ _ _	9 52			1238			5 18			7 13		7 4	
15½	Birdbrook _ _ _ _ _ ..	10 0			1246			5 26			7 22		7 12	
19½	Haverhill ... _ _ _ arr	10 8			1254			5 34			7 31		7 20	
74½	25 London (L'pool St) arr	12 38			4 52			8 40			11 23		9 19	

Miles		Week Days										Sundays	
		am			am			pm			pm		pm
25	London (L'pool St) dep	4 24	..	..	5 54	..	..	12×10	..	..	3 24	..	2 24	..	..
—	Haverhill _ _ _ _ _ dep	7 11			9 22			2 22			6 5		4 43	
3½	Birdbrook _ _	7 20			9 31			2 31			6 15		4 52	
7½	Yeldham .. _ _ _	7 28			9 39			2 39			6 23		5 2	
10	Sible and Castle Hedingham	7 35			9d51			2 45			6 30		5 9	
13½	Halstead.. _ _ _ _	7d46			9 59			2 52			6K50		5 16	
16	Earls Colne _ _ _	7 53			10 6			2 58			7 3		5 22	
17½	White Colne _ _ _	7 58			1011			3 3			7 8		5 27	
19½	Chappel & Wakes C. arr	8 2			1015			3 7			7 12		5 31	
69½	25 London (L'pool St) arr	9 57			1152			4F34			9 4		7 19	

1 On Saturdays departs Liverpool Street 2 29 pm	**F** On Saturdays arrives Liverpool Street 4 40 pm	**K** Arr 6 36 pm
b Arrives 4 minutes earlier	**g** Arrives 9 minutes earlier	**S** Saturdays only
d Arrives 5 minutes earlier		**TC** Through Carriages

BR timetable of 17th September, 1956 showing service provided after transfer of operation to Cambridge/Colchester to which places no connecting times have been shown.

Table 22 **MARK'S TEY, HALSTEAD, SUDBURY, HAVERHILL and CAMBRIDGE**

Week Days

Miles	Miles		am		am	am	am	am	am		am	am	pm		am	pm	pm	pm
					To Bury St. Edmunds arr 8 29 am (Table 23)		Through Train to Audley End arr 11E10, 10S56 am (Table 29)	Through Train Colchester to Cambridge			Except Saturdays Through Train Colchester to Cambridge	Saturdays only Through Train from Colchester	Saturdays only				Through Train Colchester to Bury St. Edmunds arr 2 58 pm (Table 23)	Through Train Colchester to Cambridge
		3 London (L'pool St) dep	..	..	4 35	6 54	..	8 30	..	..	9C33	10C30	..	..	1130	..	12L33	1N30
		3 Colchester .... ,,	..	..	6K49	7 21	..	9 48	..	..	11 47	11 47	..	..	..	..	1 49	3 2
			D		D	[D]	[D]	D	[D]		D	D	D		[D]	[D]	D	
—	—	**Mark's Tey** .. .. dep	..	..	7 27	8 21		9 56	..	..	11 58	11 58	..	..	1256	..	2 0	3 11
3½	3½	Chappel & Wakes Colne..	..	..	7 33	..		10c5	10 8	..	12 4	12 4	..	..	1 3	..	2 6	3 18
2	5½	White Colne	..	..	..	..		..	1014	..	..	..	..	..	1 8	..	..	..
3½	7	Earls Colne..........	..	..	..	..		..	1017	..	..	..	..	..	1 12	..	..	..
6	9½	**Halstead**	..	..	..	8 37		..	1023	..	..	..	..	..	1 17	..	..	..
9½	13	Sible & Castle Hedingham	..	..	..	..		..	1029	..	..	..	..	..	1 24	..	..	..
12	15½	Yeldham	..	..	..	..		..	1035	..	..	..	..	..	1 29	..	..	..
15¾	19¼	Birdbrook	..	..	..	..		..	1042	..	..	..		..	1 37	..	..	..
6¾	—	Bures	..	..	7 40	..		1011	..	..	12 11	12 11		..	..	..	2 13	3 25
11¾	—	**Sudbury** (Suffolk).. arr	..	..	7 47	..		1019	..	..	12 18	12 18		..	..	..	2 20	3 32
		dep	6 37	..	7 48	..		1024	..	..	12 18	12 18		..	..	..	2 20	3 35
14¾	—	Long Melford..........	6 44	..	7 54	..		1031	..	..	12 25	12 25		..	..	..	2 27	3d45
17¼	—	Glemsford	6 49	..	..	..		1036	..	..	12 30	12 30	..	..	..	..		3 50
18½	—	Cavendish............	6 53	..	..	..		1039	..	..	12 34	12 34	..	..	..	..		3 54
21¼	—	Clare	6 58	..	..	..		1044	..	..	12 42	12 42	..	..	..	..		3 59
23¼	—	Stoke (Suffolk).........	7 2	..		..		1049	..	..	12 46	12 46	..	..	..	..		4 3
26¼	—	Sturmer	7 8	..		..		1054	..	..	12 52	12 52	..	..	..	..		4 9
28¼	23	**Haverhill** .... arr	7 12	..		9 0	..	1059	1052	..	12 56	12 56	..	..	1 44	..		4 13
		dep	7 13	..		..	10 25	1059		..	12 57	..	1 27	..	..	2 6		4 14
34¼	29	Bartlow............ arr	7 23	..		..	10 39	1110	..	..	1 7	..	1 37	..	..	2 16		4 25
83¼	78	**29 London** (L'pool St) arr	9H 3	..		..	12b42	1Y49	..	..	4 51	..	4 51	..	..	..		..
—	—	Bartlow............ dep	7 23	..		..	..	1110	..	..	1 7	..	1 37	..	..	2 16		4 25
36¼	31	Linton	7 28	..		..	..	1114	..	..	1 12	..	1 45	..	..	2 21		4 29
39	33¾	Pampisford............	7 33	..		..	..	1120	..	..	1 17	..	1 51	..	..	2 26		..
43¼	38	Shelford .. } A	7 41	..		..	..	..	..	..	1 28	..	1 58	..	..	2 34		..
46¼	41¼	**Cambridge**.. } A .. arr	7 50	..		..	..	1135	..	..	1 38	..	2 7	..	..	2P44		4 57
101¼	96	**8 London** (King's C.) arr	10 3	..	..	..	..	1S33	..	..	..	..	4† 6	..	..	4b41		7F 6
99	93¾	4 ,, (L'pool St) ,,	9J48	..	..	..	..	1Y49	..	..	..	..	..	..	..	b4J51		..

	Week Days *continued*											Sundays									
	pm	pm		pm		pm		pm		pm		pm	pm		pm	pm	pm	pm		pm	
	Through Train Colchester to Cambridge			Through Train Ipswich dep 5 20 pm to Cambridge (Table 3)						Through Train from Colchester		Through Train from Colchester	Through Train to Audley End arr 5 30 pm (Table 29)				Through Train to Audley End arr 7 29 pm (Table 29)				
3 London (L'pool St) dep	2 30	..	..	4Q59	..	5U45	..	6E45	..	8C30	..	2 21	..	..	3 19	4 45	..	6 20	..	8 15	..
3 Colchester .... ,,	4 36	..	..	5 52	..	6 19	..	7 32	..	9 50	..	3 51	..	..	5 12	6 6	..	..	..	8 59	..
	D	D		D		D		D		D		D	[D]		D	D	[D]	D		D	
Mark's Tey .. .. dep	4 45	..	..	6 7	..	7 6	..	8 15	..	9 58	..	3 59	..	..	5 27	6 21	..	7 59	..	9 52	..
Chappel & Wakes Colne..	4 51	4 55	..	6 13	..	7 13	..	..	..	10 4	..	..		..	..	..		..	..	..	..
White Colne	..	5 1	..	..	..	..	..	..	..	..	..	..		..	..	..		..	..	..	..
Earls Colne..........	..	5 4	..	..	..	7 20	..	..	..	..	..	..		..	..	..		..	..	..	..
Halstead	..	5 10	..	..	..	7 26	..	..	..	..	..	..		..	..	..		..	..	..	..
Sible & Castle Hedingham	..	5 16	..	..	..	7 32	..	..	..	..	..	..		..	..	..		..	..	..	..
Yeldham	..	5 22	..	..	..	7 38	..	..	..	..	..	..		..	..	..		..	..	..	..
Birdbrook	..	5 29	..	..	..	7 45	..	..	..	..	..	..		..	..	..		..	..	..	..
Bures	4 58	..	..	6 20	..	..	..	8 26	..	1011	..	4 11		..	5 38	6 32		8 10	..	10 3	..
Sudbury (Suffolk).. arr	5 5	..	..	6 27	..	..	..	8 34	..	1020	..	4 18		..	5 46	6 40		8 18	..	1011	..
dep	5 6	..	..	6 29	..	..	..	..	..		..	..		..	..	..		..	..	..	..
Long Melford..........	5 12	..	..	6g41	..	..	..	..	..		..	..		..	..	..		..	..	..	..
Glemsford	5 17	..	..	6 46	..	..	..	..	..		..	..		..	..	..		..	..	..	..
Cavendish............	5 21	..	..	6 49	..	..	..	..	..		..	..		..	..	..		..	..	..	..
Clare	5 27	..	..	6 54	..	..	..	..	..		..	..		..	..	..		..	..	..	..
Stoke (Suffolk).........	5 31	..	..	6 59	..	..	..	..	..		..	..		..	..	..		..	..	..	..
Sturmer	5 37	..	..	7 4	..	..	..	..	..		..	..		..	..	..		..	..	..	..
Haverhill .... arr	5 41	5 37	..	7 9	..	7 53	..	..	..		..	..		..	..	..		..	..	..	..
dep	5 43		..	7 9	..	7 53	..	..	..		..	..	5 5	..	..	..	7 4	..	..	..	..
Bartlow............ arr	5 53	..	..	7 19	..	8 3	..	..	..		..	..	..	..	..	..	..	..	..	..	..
29 London (L'pool St) arr	7G56	..	..	..	..	11 29	..	..	..	..	..	..	6b46	..	..	..	9b10	..	..	..	..
Bartlow............ dep	5 53	..	..	7 19	..	8 11	..	..	..	..	..	..	..	..	..	..	..	..	..	..	..
Linton	5 58	..	..	7 24	..	8 15	..	..	..	..	..	..	..	..	..	..	..	..	..	..	..
Pampisford............	6 3	..	..	7 29	..	..	..	..	..	..	..	..	..	..	..	..	..	..	..	..	..
Shelford .. } A	6 11	..	..	7 37	..	8 27	..	..	..	..	..	..	..	..	..	..	..	..	..	..	..
Cambridge.. } A .. arr	6 21	..	..	7B46	..	8 35	..	..	..	..	..	..	..	..	..	..	..	..	..	..	..
8 London (King's C.) arr	..	..	..	9V25	..	11n 4	..	..	..	..	..	..	..	..	..	..	..	..	..	..	..
4 ,, (L'pool St) ,,	8T49	..	..	..	..	11Z29	..	..	..	..	..	..	..	..	..	..	..	..	..	..	..

D Diesel Train
[D] Diesel Train. Second class only

† Second class only
A For other trains between Shelford and Cambridge, see Table 4
B On Saturdays arr 7 49 pm
b First and Second class
C Via Colchester
c Arr 3 minutes *earlier*
d Arr 4 minutes *earlier*

E Except Saturdays
F On Saturdays arr 7†7 pm
G On Saturdays 4 minutes later
g Arr 6 minutes *earlier*
H On Saturdays 10 minutes later
J Via Shelford
K On Saturdays dep 6 45 am
L Saturdays only. Via Colchester
N Via Colchester. On Saturdays dep 1 33 pm

n Second class only Mondays to Fridays
P On Saturdays arr 2 40 pm
Q On Saturdays dep 4C30 pm
T On Fridays arr 8 38 pm
U On Saturdays dep 5 30 pm
V On Saturdays arr 10 7 pm
Y On Saturdays arr 1 44 pm
Z On Saturdays arr 10 5 pm

Table 23—see page 213

Timetable for service of diesel Rail-buses and Multiple-Units introduced 12.9.60: connections off the CV line at both Chappel and Haverhill have now been included, but no Sunday trains now run on the CV line.

Table 22— *continued*

CAMBRIDGE, HAVERHILL, SUDBURY, HALSTEAD and MARK'S TEY

Week Days

Miles	Miles		am	am	am	am		am	am	am	am		am	am	am		pm	pm	pm
						Through Train Bury St. Edmunds dep 7 45 am to Mark's Tey (Table 23)			On Mondays to Fridays Through Train Cambridge to Colchester	Through Train from Audley End dep 9 30 am (Table 29)			Through Train Cambridge to Colchester	Saturdays only			Saturdays only Through Train to Colchester		Through Train Cambridge to Colchester
		4 London (L'pool St) dep	..	4J20	..	..	..	..	5J50	..	..	..	9P50	..	11S20	..	..	..	12U20
		8 „ (King's C.) „												1030	11E 5				12S25
			D	[D]	[D]	D		[D]	D	[D]	[D]		D		D			D	D
—	—	**Cambridge** } A .... dep	..	6 35	..	..	..	..	8 21	..	..	..	1140	1233	1 25	..	..	..	2 35
3¼	3¼	Shelford .... }		6 42					8 27				1146		1 31				2 41
7½	7½	Pampisford	..	6 50	..	..	..	..	8 34	..	..	..	1153	..	1 38	..	..	..	2 48
10½	10½	Linton		6 56					8 40				1159		1 44				2 54
12¼	12¼	Bartlow arr	..	7 0	..	..	..	..	8 44	..	..	..	12 3	..	1 48	..	..	..	2 58
—	—	**29 London** (L'pool St) dep								8b20			9 50						12K20
—	—	Bartlow dep	..	7 1	..	..	..	..	8 45	9 47	..	..	12 4	..	1 49	..	..	..	2 58
18¼	18¼	**Haverhill** arr		7 11					8 55	10 2			1214	1 1	1 59				3 9
		Haverhill dep	..	..	7 24	..	..	9 5	8 57		11 0	..	1215		2 0	..	2 3	3 20	3 15
20¼	—	Sturmer							9 2		11 4		1219		2 4				3 20
23½	—	Stoke (Suffolk)	..	..	..	..	..	..	9 7		11 9	..	1225		2 10	..	..	..	3 25
25½	—	Clare							9 12		1113		1230		2 15				3 30
28	—	Cavendish	..	..	..	..	..	..	9 18		1117	..	1235		2 21	..	..	..	3 35
29¾	—	Glemsford							9 22		1120		1139		2 24				3 39
31¾	—	Long Melford	..	..	..	8 15	..	..	9 28		1125	..	1244	..	2c32	..	..	..	3 44
34¾	—	**Sudbury** (Suffolk) arr				8 21			9 34		1130		1250		2 38				3 50
		Sudbury (Suffolk) dep	7 1	..	..	8 22	..	..	9 35		1131	..	1250	..	..	..	..	..	3 50
39¾	—	Bures	7 8			8 29			9 43		1139		1258						3 58
—	22	Birdbrook	..	..	7 32	..	..	9 12	..		..	..	..	..	..	..	2 10	3 27	..
—	25¾	Yeldham			7 39			9 19									2 17	3 34	
—	28½	Sible & Castle Hedingham	..	..	7 44	..	..	9 24	..		..	..	..	..	..	..	2 22	3 39	..
—	31¾	**Halstead**			7 51			9 31									2 29	3 46	
—	34	Earls Colne	..	..	7 56	..	..	9 36	..		..	..	..	..	..	..	2 34	3 51	..
—	35½	White Colne						9 39									2 37	3 54	
43	37¾	Chappel & Wakes Colne	7 16	..	8 4	8 37	..	9 46	10N 4		1144	..	1 5	..	..	..	2 42	4 1	4 5
46½	41½	**Mark's Tey** arr	7 22		8 12	8 43			10 10		1150		1 12				2 48		4 12
51½	46½	3 Colchester arr	..	..	8b27	8 57	..	..	10H35	..	1L 1	..	1 20	..	..	..	3 3	..	4 21
93¾	88	3 London (L'pool St) „	8 46			10 0			11G51				2n51				4C30		5 43

Week Days— *continued* / **Sundays**

	pm	pm		pm	pm		pm		pm		pm		pm	pm	pm		pm	pm		pm		pm
	Week Days												Sundays									
	Through Train Bury St. Edmunds dep 4 23 pm to Colchester (Table 23)	From Bury St. Edmunds dep 5 49 pm (Table 23)					Through Train to Colchester		Through Train from Audley End dep 7 0 pm (Table 29)		Through Train Cambridge to Colchester		Through Train from Audley End dep 3 51 pm (Table 29)				Through Train from Audley End dep 5 40 pm (Table 29)					Through Train to Ipswich arr 11 9 pm (Table 3)
4 London (L'pool St) dep	..	..	..	3J20	..	..	..	..	..	..	5V57	..	..	..	..	..	..	..	..	..	..	..
8 „ (King's C.) „				3 5							5S40											
	D				D				[D]		D		[D]	D	D		[D]	D		D		D
Cambridge } A .... dep	..	..	..	5 24	..	..	..	..	..	..	7 39	..	..	..	..	..	..	..	..	..	..	..
Shelford .... }				5 31							7 45											
Pampisford	..	..	..	5 39	..	..	..	..	..	..	7 52	..	..	..	..	..	..	..	..	..	..	..
Linton				5 46							7 58											
Bartlow arr	..	..	..	5 51	..	..	..	..	..	..	8 2	..	..	..	..	..	..	..	..	..	..	..
29 London (L'pool St) dep				3 20					5b54		5 54		2b20				3b20					
Bartlow dep	..	..	..	5 55	..	..	..	..	7 16	..	8 10	..	..	..	..	..	..	..	..	..	..	..
Haverhill arr				6 7					7 31		8 20		4 16				6 5					
Haverhill dep	..	..	..	6 9	6 13	..	..	..	..	..	8 24	..	..	..	..	..	..	..	..	..	..	..
Sturmer				6 12							8 28											
Stoke (Suffolk)	..	..	..	6 18	..	..	..	..	..	..	8 34	..	..	..	..	..	..	..	..	..	..	..
Clare				6 23							8 38											
Cavendish	..	..	..	6 29	..	..	..	..	..	..	8 44	..	..	..	..	..	..	..	..	..	..	..
Glemsford				6 32							8 47											
Long Melford	4 52	6 18	..	6 39	..	..	..	..	..	..	8 53	..	..	..	..	..	..	..	..	..	..	..
Sudbury (Suffolk) arr	4 58	6 24		6 47							8 59											
Sudbury (Suffolk) dep	5 7	..	..	..	..	..	7 10	..	..	..	9 0	..	..	4 52	5 50	..	..	7 30	..	8 44	..	10 16
Bures							7 18				9 7			4 59	5 58			7 37		8 51		
Birdbrook	..	..	..	..	6 20	..	..	..	..	..	..	..	..	..	..	..	..	..	..	..	..	..
Yeldham					6 27																	
Sible & Castle Hedingham	..	..	..	..	6 32	..	..	..	..	..	..	..	..	..	..	..	..	..	..	..	..	..
Halstead					6 39																	
Earls Colne	..	..	..	..	6 44	..	..	..	..	..	..	..	..	..	..	..	..	..	..	..	..	..
White Colne					6F47																	
Chappel & Wakes Colne	..	..	..	..	6 54	..	7 27	..	..	..	9c18	..	..	..	..	..	..	..	..	..	..	..
Mark's Tey arr	5 25				7 1		7 34				9 24			5 12	6 10			7 50		9 4		10 34
3 Colchester arr	5 33	..	..	..	7E13	..	7 55	..	..	..	9 32	..	..	..	6 32	..	..	8 10	..	10 1	..	10 42
3 London (L'pool St) „	7 44				9 7		9 7				12a27			7 3	8 0			9 53		1054		12a30

D Diesel Train
[D] Diesel Train. Second class only

A For other trains between Shelford and Cambridge, see Table 4
a am
b First and Second class
C Via Colchester
c Arr 3 minutes *earlier*
E Except Saturdays

F Calls to set down passengers only
G On Saturdays arr 11 30 am
H On Saturdays arr 10 53 am
J Via Shelford
K On Saturdays dep 12 14 pm
L First and Second class. On Saturdays arr 12 52 pm
N Arr 9 51 am

n On Saturdays arr 2 38 pm
P On Mondays to Fridays via Shelford
S Saturdays only
U On Saturdays dep 12 24 pm via Shelford
V Via Shelford. On Saturdays dep 5 54 pm via Cambridge

Table 23—see page 213

Appendix D

SUMMARY TABLE OF THE LOCOMOTIVES USED ON THE COLNE VALLEY RAILWAY

Colne Valley Rly. No	Name	Builder	Makers No.	Date Built	Date Acq'd	TYPE	WHEELS: Driving	Others	CYLS:	Htg. Surf. Sq. feet	Grate: Sq. feet	REMARKS
1	CAM	Geo. England		c1854	Hired only	2-4-0T	3' 8"	2' 9"	11 x 17			Hired from Mr. Munro the Contractor. Used after on extension work to Haverhill.
1	COLNE	Geo. England		c1854	1860	2-4-0T	3' 8"	2' 9"	11 x 17			
?	?	Laird & Kitson	32	1845	1861	2-4-0	4' 6"	3' 0"	14 x 18			Second-hand from the Eastern Counties Railway.
?	?	Sharp Roberts		1844	1860	2-2-2W.T	5' 6"	3' 8"	15 x 22			Second-hand from the London, Brighton & South Coast Rly. The dimensions are those whilst on the Colne Valley Railway.
1	BREWSTER	Manning Wardle	34	1860	1860	2-4-0T	5' 0"	3' 9"	14 x 18	720	9.5	Purchased by Chas. Brewster, Esq.
1	COLNE	Manning Wardle	59	1862	1862	2-4-0T	5' 0"	3' 9"	14 x 18	720	9.5	Loaned by him to the Company.
1	HALSTEAD	Manning Wardle	61	1863	1863	2-4-0T	5' 0"	3' 9"	14 x 18	720	9.5	
1	HAVERHILL	Neilson & Co.	2204	1877	1877	0-4-2T	5' 3"	3' 7"	15 x 22	752.6	12.7	Twice rebuilt. Survived to LNER.
1		Sharp Stewart	2358	1873	1878	0-6-0T	3' 6"	—	16¼ x 20	823.5	10.8	Second-hand from Cornish Mineral Rly. (No. 10). Sold 1889 to S. Hetton Colliery Co. Worked until 1948.
2		Beyer Peacock	190	1860	c1883	0-4-2ST	5' 0"	3' 6"	16 x 24	925	13	Originally N. London Rly No. 42 Bought from Whitehaven Coll'y Co Sold 1894 to S. Hetton Coll'y Co.
2	HALSTEAD	Hawthorn Leslie	2079	1887	1887	2-4-2T	5' 1"	3' 2"	16 x 24	919		All survived to L.N.E.R.
3	COLNE	Hawthorn Leslie	2080	1887	1887	2-4-2T	5' 1"	3' 2"	16 x 24	919		
4	HEDINGHAM	Hawthorn Leslie	2283	1894	1894	2-4-2T	5' 1"	3' 2"	16 x 24	919		Heating surface increased to 1038.5 sq. ft. when rebuilt.
5		Hudswell Clarke	836	1908	1908	0-6-2T	4' 6"	3' 8"	16 x 24	974	14.65	Survived to L.N.E.R.

Appendix E

Working arrangements vis-a-vis Great Eastern and Colne Valley & Halstead Railways

Extracts from GER Appendix to the Working Timetable, 1921.

CHAPPEL STATION

Shunting Operations

Whenever it is necessary to shunt Trucks on to the Colne Valley Single Line at Chappel Station, care must be taken that the Trucks are not pushed beyond the Up Home Signal, and that in every case a Break Van is at the Haverhill end of the Wagons.

"Calling on" Signal

When the "Calling on" Signal (fixed on the C.V. Branch Up Home Signal Post) is lowered it will be the authority for the Driver of a Colne Valley Passenger train to draw his train slowly past the Home Signal, as far as the Points leading to the Colne Valley Siding, or as far as the Points (near the Signal Box) leading from the Down to the Up Line, as may be most convenient. The lowering of this Signal will also be the authority for the Driver of a Colne Valley **Goods** train to draw his train slowly past the Home Signal, either for the purpose of going direct into the Goods Yard, or of stopping short of the Points leading to the Goods Yard, as may be most convenient.

Working of C.V. Carriage Trains from Haverhill C.V. Junction to Haverhill G.E. Station

C.V. Carriage trains requiring to run to Haverhill G.E. Station are to be run **engine first** from the Colne Valley Junction to the G.E. Station; the engine to be run round its train at the latter Station.

List of Engine Whistles for Stations, Junctions and Sidings.

Haverhill Junction ......To or from Sudbury Line ...... **1** distinct sound
To or from C.V. Line .... **2** distinct sounds

Chappel and   G.E. Line .... **1** distinct sound
Wake's Colne ....
                    To or from
                    G.E. Line and C.V. Line ... **3** distinct sounds

In this notice "Haverhill Junc" refers to the junction 15 ch. east of Haverhill GE station at the point where the Sudbury and Colne Valley lines separate; and not the junction as shown with this name in the RCH diagram shown on page 18.

98

NOTE:

As an indication that a Goods or Mineral train, which is booked to call at a Station or Siding, has no Wagons or Goods to leave and will not stop if the Station Staff, or man in charge of the Siding, gives a right-away Hand-signal. In the absence of a Hand-signal the train must be stopped as booked.	**2 crows.** *To be given on approaching the Station or Siding.*
As an indication that the whole of the train which has been shunted into a Refuge Siding is clear of the Safety Points.	**1 crow.**

There was an arrangement between the Companies for the mutual exchange of telegrams.

The Great Eastern issued through tickets from Liverpool Street to all Colne Valley line stations: and also to Halstead from Cambridge, Ipswich and Norwich.

There was mutual acceptance of Cheap Week-end tickets between the two railways in accordance with the arrangements set out in the following notice:

CHEAP WEEK-END TICKETS
First, Second (where applicable) and Third Class
ARE (WITH A FEW EXCEPTIONS) ISSUED

EVERY SATURDAY
BETWEEN

ANY TWO GREAT EASTERN STATIONS,
(INCLUDING JOINT LINE STATIONS), ALSO BETWEEN

GREAT EASTERN STATIONS
(INCLUDING JOINT LINE STATIONS) AND STATIONS ON

Barry	Great Northern	Midland & Great Northern Joint
Brecon and Merthyr	Great Northern and Great	Midland & South Western Junc.
Cambrian	Eastern Joint	Neath and Brecon
Cheshire Lines Committee	Great Western	Norfolk and Suffolk Joint
Cockermouth, Keswick and	Hull and Barnsley	North Eastern
Penrith	Knott End	North London
Colne Valley and Halstead	Lancashire and Yorkshire	Rhymney
East London Joint Committee (including New Cross, L.B. & S.C. Rly.)	London and North Western	Stratford-upon-Avon & Mid. Jne.
	London and South Western	Taff Vale
	(with certain exceptions)	Wirral
Furness	Maryport and Carlisle	
Great Central (including Joint Lines)	Midland (excluding London, Tilbury & Southend section)	and certain other Railways.

At a SINGLE FARE and a THIRD.
Minimum Fare—First Class, 4s. 0d.; Second Class, 3s. 0d.; Third Class, 2s. 6d. Fractional parts of a Penny will be charged as a Penny.

The Tickets are issued by any Train on Saturdays, and are available for return by any Train on the Sunday at or after 6.0 a.m. (if train service permits) or Monday following date of issue.

These Cheap Tickets are (with a few exceptions) issued at the Liverpool Street fares between Suburban Stations and Stations below Shelford and Mark's Tey.

There was a similar reciprocal arrangement in respect of Colne Valley Fortnightly return tickets issued from Halstead and Haverhill (CV) stations at reduced rates to most of the "watering-places" [sic] on the Essex, Suffolk and Norfolk coasts, which also held good for Friday to Tuesday tickets for a visit to the Sea-Side [sic].

On Sundays Day return tickets at a single fare were issued between all Colne Valley line stations, and also to and from all Great Eastern stations within the area of the former "Eastern Union" railway: e.g. Sudbury, Colchester, Harwich, Ipswich, Bury St Edmunds, Norwich and Woodbridge, subject to availability of trains: the arrangement came to an end during the 1914–1918 war.

Appendix F
Today's Colne Valley Railway

The Colne Valley Railway is a re-creation of a typical branch line of the Victorian era. As such, it forms a microcosm of the railway scene of times past, a fascinating glimpse of a system of transportation which revolutionised this country and indeed much of the world from the 1840s to the 1930s.

Early in 1972, local railway enthusiasts formed the Colne Valley Railway Preservation Society with the object of rebuilding as much as possible of the old Colne Valley & Halstead Railway on a one mile section of the original track bed.

When purchased, the site resembled a forest with dense growth of bushes and trees. This had to be cleared before any building or track laying could commence, for the original track had been lifted ten years earlier. No buildings or platforms existed on the site as the length of line lay between two former stations.

Today, after much hard work by the Society, the Colne Valley Railway comprises two platforms, each with an authentic railway station building. There is a dock where merchandise and cattle could be handled, a signal box, water crane, signals and other railway equipment. Within, there are a bookshop and a reconstruction of an early 1900s ticket and booking office.

Meals and refreshments are served each day in the restaurant car, and there is a 3½ acre picnic area by the River Colne.

Further information may be obtained from Colne Valley Railway Co., Ltd., Castle Hedingham Station, Yeldham Road, Castle Hedingham, Halstead, Essex CO9 3DZ, or Telephone: Hedingham (0787) 61174.